The Trial of Supercrip (And the Conviction of Narrative Prosthesis)

James Faumuina

Published by Imagine Pacific, 2023.

THE TRIAL OF SUPERCRIP (AND THE CONVICTION OF NARRATIVE PROSTHESIS)

First edition. December 31, 2023.

Copyright © 2023 James Faumuina.

ISBN: 979-8224252022

Written by James Faumuina.

Table of Contents

THE TRIAL OF SUPERCRIP

And The Conviction of Narrative Prothesis

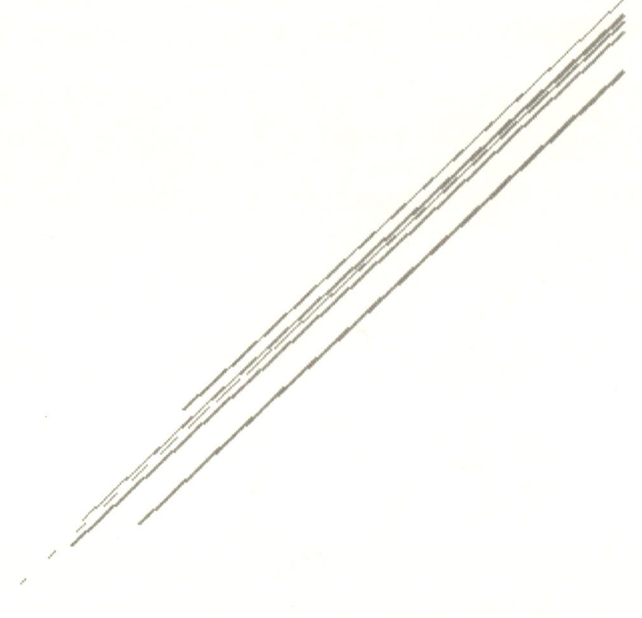

BY
JAMES E. FAUMUINA, MBA, MPA

For my brothers Johnny and Joey, the lens they shared is the lens I am starting to understand.

Preface

In my book "The Trial of Supercrip (And the Conviction of Narrative Prosthesis)," I will attempt to present my personal exploration of disability, identity, and societal tropes. Through the story of Cormac and Supercrip, readers are invited to consider the ways in which societal norms and expectations shape our understanding of ourselves and others.

The story of Cormac and Supercrip is one that is intended to be thought-provoking and emotionally engaging. As readers follow the journey of these two characters, they will be confronted with complex issues related to disability, identity, and defined roles. The play encourages readers to think critically about these issues, question their own assumptions, and develop a genuine perspective.

Thank You for choosing to enter the world of Cormac and Supercrip.

FORWARD:

The concept for Supercrip came from a writing assignment I had while attending Graduate School. The assignment was part of a course called, Disabilities Studies. I had no idea what exactly Disabilities Studies were, but I needed to consume a few credits in order to retain my active standing as I awaited the registration period for a Ph.D. program, I had my hopes on. Prior to taking this course, I had no idea what it had in store for me. However, after taking it, I don't think I will be able to perceive disabilities the same way. I have been exposed to a new language in this discipline and my perspective of my own disability, as well as my perspective of those with disabilities, has been radically changed forever. The concept of the disabilities lens will be addressed in the play Supercrip; however, it can also be found as part of the jargon associated with Disabilities Studies.

I am a disabled veteran, and I have family members who are disabled. It may seem strange to claim representation in the disabled community, but after reading "Supercrip" and its collection of essays in this book, I hope you will realize that the reality is that we will all eventually either care for someone with a disability or become disabled ourselves. It is an inevitability that comes with age, illness, and sometimes random chance. I used creative narrative to illustrate the universe of Disabled Studies. First as an economy of scale that utilized Disabilities Studies terms and concepts, second to provide a character driven story with disability, and third to illuminate the tropes commonly expressed in media and observed in daily publicized story lines regardless of where you get your news from.

In addition to the play, the Compendium is also provided as an extended epilogue that allows the reader to explore the concepts presented in Supercrip more fully and specifically per essay.

INTRODUCTION:

The societal tropes used as a narrative for disabled people are often based on informational bias, stereotyped convenience, and comfortable ignorance whereupon stigma is empowered by a desire to sustain the established standard for normalcy and isolation of anything considered abnormal.

The story you are about to read is a creative narrative depiction of the thesis provided. The story of Cormac and Supercrip could be considered a character study in many of the terms and concepts from the field of Disabilities Studies. The protagonist in this story has a disability, however, there is no emphasis on the type of disability. Intentionally, that detail is left out to allow anyone with a disability to play the role of Cormac. The name of Cormac was chosen based on the author Cormac McCarthy. His flagrant abuse of the character he called the "imbecile" in his work Blood Meridian (1) speaks to the type of oppression and devaluation disabled people experience in their daily life with stigmas, isolation, and cruelty. I found no better means to pay him back and right these wrongs by naming the title character in this disabled anti-hero story after him.

Supercrip is the alter-ego of Cormac. He is a larger-than-life character with the appearance of a superhero, but the ethos of a supervillain. Where in many media depictions the transition from disabled to hero was seen as overcoming a disability, in this story the transition from disabled to superhero normally results in chaos. Cormac intentionally retains his identity at the cost of his freedom because of his principles and values system.

Herein, lies the mark of the heroism in the form of ethical, honest, and a real disabled identity. Numerous times, Supercrip will tempt Cormac into using his superpowers to invoke "justice", however Cormac will continue to retain the moral compass and avoid abandoning his disabled identity. The journey Cormac and Supercrip go through include reminiscing their disabled youth, adolescence, and eventually radical advocacy.

This production is minimalist with only two physical actors, voices from off stage, no set design with only a few tables, chair, cot, and a few props. The narration is done with the audience in order to utilize the device of "breaking the fourth wall." The use of the spotlight and stage lighting also plays a significant role in the pace and emphasis of the performance. The use of footnotes is frequent in the script. The notes are all located at the end of each respective page and quotations are mostly taken from the substantive authors in Disabilities Studies as references.

The story of Cormac and Supercrip test the boundaries of traditional superhero stories. It introduces some essential disabilities studies vernacular, and it attempts to gage the heart of the thesis by pointing out the varied opinion of what is just and what is normal; ensuring that it is all viewed through the disabilities' lens.

CAST OF CHARACTERS:

- CORMAC - DISABLED DEFENDANT ON TRIAL

- SUPERCRIP - ABLE-BODIED SUPER POWERED ALTER-EGO OF CORMAC

- VOICES OFF STAGE:

- AIDE - MONITORING CORMAC/ SUPERCRIP IN THE INSTITUTION

- JEN - HIGH SCHOOL CRUSH

- JUDGE - PRESIDING JUDGE OVER TRIAL

- JURY FOREMAN - PROVIDES CORMAC'S SENTENCE

- KIDS - VOICES OF CLASSMATES

- LOUDSPEAKER - GIVES ALERTS IN THE GENETICS LAB

- MOM - MOTHER OF CORMAC/SUPERCRIP

- POLICE - INTERCEPTS CORMAC AT THE GENETICS LAB

- TEACHER - MS. B; CORMACS FIRST EXPERIENCE WITH A TEACHER/

AUTHORITY

- TV VOICES - (NEWSCASTER, ADVERTISEMENT, INTERVIEWEE)

<u>ACT I</u>

The story begins with a man on trial named Cormac. He is preparing to receive the sentence for crimes he has committed. Cormac has an alter ego that goes by the moniker of Supercrip. Cormac is on trial for murder, destruction of property and domestic terrorism.

Sitting in his chair alone behind an unfolded table, that is serving the function of the defendant's desk, Cormac is sitting with his head in his hands awaiting the verdict to be read. Cormac is a man in his early thirties, his skin is a dark complexion, he is considered obesely overweight, (2) he has visually apparent thick lensed glasses and has visual signs of impairment from his limping gaunt and leaning posture. His impairment does not affect his speech, but it does impact his mobility. He requires a cane for support at times, and he can speak clearly but sometimes he takes his time when responding to others in normal conversations. (3)

A judge's voice is heard from off-stage. He is preparing to pass sentence upon Cormac and is going to ask him if there is anything he wishes to say before sentencing. The opening monologue will occur with Cormac" breaking the fourth wall" so the audience can be brought into the story. During the performance, many times the stage lights will go down and then be brought back up as Cormac's.

alter-ego Supercrip trades off duties with Cormac as the narrator. (4)

<u>Scene I: The Courtroom</u>

Situated center stage, facing the audience, is a chair and a folding table, Cormac will start the scene sitting in the chair behind the table facing the audience. Off-Stage there will be two voices: The Judge and The Jury Foreman to start the scene.

JUDGE: (Off Stage.) Does the jury have a verdict?

JURY FOREMAN: (Off stage.) Yes, your honor.

JUDGE: Very well bring it to me. (Pause.) Will the defendant please rise. Please be prepared to hear the verdict from your peers. (Cormac rises from his seat.)

JUDGE: Mr. Cormac, a jury of your peers have found you guilty of first-degree murder and domestic terrorism. (Cormac looks out into the audience. The verdict has just set in, and he begins to sit down.)

JUDGE: Mr. Cormac please keep standing. I have taken some time to think about this case, and before I pass sentence I would like to hear if there is anything you want to say.

(Cormac shakes his head side to side to nonverbally inform the judge he does not and proceeds to sit down. Lights go down. In the darkness, Cormac exits stage

left at the same time Supercrip enters stage right. Lights come back up and Supercrip has switched places with Cormac and is now standing behind the desk in front of the chair, facing the audience, and preparing to respond to the judge.)

SUPERCRIP: Hold on your honor... (Pause.) I have a few things I want to say. First, don't you think this is all a bit cliche? I mean c'mon? Look at how the system finds comfort in sending away guys like me... I mean... him (Points Behind him.) ... Ah you know what I mean! (5)

(Supercrip has a muscular build, his skin complexion is white, he has "SC" embroidered on his flowing red cape, mirror shades, thigh-high white boots and a sequenced codpiece that fits way too snug. His voice is deep with a rich- nasally tint that tends to leave off words with a long draw and over pronunciation occasionally. His first impression is that he hits all the possible superhero tropes imaginable, and he just went on a spending spree at the super-hero apparel outlet.)

JUDGE: Don't do that again Mr. Cormac! Bailiff! Please attend to Mr. Cormac and the other guy too as well. (Addresses his request to Supercrip.) Could you please bring back Mr. Cormac?

(Lights go out and Supercrip exits stage left in the darkness. Cormac enters stage right in the dark, he positions at the foot of the stage.

Lights come on. Cormac has reappeared and starts speaking to the audience. The "Fourth Wall" (6) has been broken. The audience is now part of the play. Cormac and Supercrip will tradeoff narrating to the audience throughout the rest of the play.)

CORMAC: Oh hello, yes, you guessed it (Frail tone). I can switch into that guy (Points in direction to the

back of the stage.) whenever I want to. As you can see by now, they are going to pass judgement on me... For what you might ask? Well... I killed someone...

Actually, I killed some people is a more accurate way of putting it. (Slight giggle and voice in a lighter tone.) Oh... I'm guilty. I did it.

(Begins to walk using his cane for assistance, he walks around the stage toward the desk and looks behind his shoulder than back at the audience.)

CORMAC: I know what else you're thinking.... Why not just switch into the other guy and fly off?

(Looks back at the desk and chair.)

CORMAC: Oh, the other guy... Geez, you are all dying to call him by his superhero name... (Hums the words and a tune that sounds like.) "Tun Tah Dah" Supercrip!"

(Cormac makes a flying motion, does a couple of superhero poses for the audience.)

CORMAC: Why? ... Because I am trying to go to jail. That's why! (Frustrated.) Be honest. This is the only way I am going to get your attention. I am not the first disabled person to stage a radical protest I Assure you. (7) (With a sense of astonishment.) What? You haven't heard about the summer of 2003 when six people starved themselves for twenty-two days or the 504 protests in the 70's? (8) ... That's the point!... Not enough people have.

(Cormac walks back to his chair and sits down. Puts his head back in his hands. Spotlight shines on Cormac. Voice of Judge can be heard from off the stage.)

JUDGE: Mr. Cormac... You were informed before this preceding started...weren't you? Counsel, please remind your client, another attempt like that crap he pulled, and you will be held in contempt with your client!

(Lights go off, Cormac exits stage right. Supercrip enters stage left simultaneously and returns to the seat and sits. Lights go on and we have Supercrip sitting in the chair giving the middle finger to the side of the stage where the voice came from.)

SUPERCRIP: Umm (Sarcastic tone.) Your honor let me explain.

(Supercrip points his index finger and thumb up in the shape of a gun toward the voice from off- stage and makes a shooting gesture and cheesy "ZIP" sound.)

SUPERCRIP: That will hold you for now.

(Voice of Judge panicked yelling backstage.)

JUDGE: I can't move... Hey... Hey... Can't... Move!

(Points to the crowd again and makes "ZING" sound.)

SUPERCRIP: Ah Yeah ... And now you can't talk. I

need you to listen for a little while please. It might change your mind (Looks at the crowd with sarcasm.) ... Probably won't but it's worth a shot

(Shooting gesture with his finger again.)... It all started in grade school.

(Lights out.)

END SCENE I

Scene II: Childhood Bedroom

Lights come back up. Cormac is sitting on the floor; he is laying on the ground on his stomach watching television. There is no actual TV, he is laying with his feet toward the rear of the stage, and he is looking out toward the audience as if they were the Television Set. The room serves as his safe space. (9) He hears his name called to him by his mother off stage.

MOM: Cormac!... Cormac!... Get ready it's time for school honey! Need Help putting your shoes on? (10)

(Irritated...yelling to her.)

CORMAC: I'm not a baby mom!

(To the side of the stage enters Supercrip stage left strolling with his hands in his pockets. He looks at Cormac. He is shaking his head as he is watching Cormac laying on the ground watching TV. Supercrip looks to the audience to start addressing them.)

SUPERCRIP: Television is such crap! Look at what we are subjected to watching.

(Shaking his head, looks back at Cormac and then looks back at the audience to start addressing them again.)

SUPERCRIP: It's all Bull Shit, they love to portray us as two-dimensional mannequins (11)... Leaves kids like him (Points to Cormac.) to believe we are all pity cases, or we are just plain helpless in need of saving.(12)

(Shaking his head, looks at Cormac and then looks at the audience.)

SUPERCRIP: I mean look at this kid... He's getting fucked up as we speak.

(Turns and looks at Cormac. Who has now proceeded to lay pronate on his stomach and pretending he is flying.)

SUPERCRIP: If he only knew...

(Lights slowly fade out to black.)

END SCENE II

SCENE III: THE CLASSROOM

Lights come back on but they are low. Spotlight is on the middle of the stage where there is a circle of chairs; five chairs spaced wide enough to see between them. The chair positioning serves as a metaphor (13) for a cell. Slumped in the center chair is Cormac and he is starting his first day of his new school. Voice from off stage is his Kindergarten Teacher, Ms. B.

Ms. B: Ok kids let's all form a circle around our newest student Cormac. Make sure you give him space and be polite when you first meet him. He is not like any of the other kids in our class.

(Voice changes to an overly syrupy sweet tone.)

MS. B: He is such an exceptional 'lil boy. (14)

(Lights still low, but now Cormac is having discussions with the empty chairs, this is done to give the audience the impression there are people sitting in them. He is having playful and jovial interactions as evidenced by his hands and head gestures. No words are said, only acting out as if there were a discussion being had. Then voices of kids are heard off stage.)

KIDS: What's wrong with your legs?... How do you go pee?... Do they give you a dog to help you if you pass out? (15)

(Spotlight then shines on the right side of the stage, and Supercrip, as if he was a bird landing from flight, leaps into the light from the right side of the curtain. He addresses the audience.)

SUPERCRIP: I think you can see the educational options weren't great for dear Cormac. He had the choice to stick it out with these moron able bodied kids... Or go to special ed! They basically didn't know what to do with him, but it was obvious whatever decision they made it was going to impact him for life! (16)

(Spotlight goes back on Cormac, he is waving bye as he continues to sit slumped in his chair. His eyes are following the imaginary images across the stage as the exit to the right. After a few seconds, lights go low on Cormac as he is sitting in the chair. Ringing Sound of a Telephone is heard. Voices come from off-stage.)

MS. B: Oh hello, is this Cormac's mom. Yes... Um... We need to consider moving Cormac to special education... I know... I know... Yes, he is already reading at 2nd grade level... And yes... I know... He does know his pluses and minuses ...And most of the States... Then why you ask? Why? Because...

(Cormac grinning at the audience as she says it.)

MS. B: He's... Exceptional!

(Spotlight stays on Supercrip. Lights go off on Cormac. In the dark, Cormac lays on the ground in the middle of the circle of chairs. Lights come back on and Cormac is crouched over with his hands covering his head as if he was trying to protect himself from getting kicked.)

CORMAC: Stop... Stop... Don't! Why are you doing this! Stop... Stop!

(Lights fade with only a faint light barely on Cormac laying down beaten. Another spotlight shines on Supercrip as he walks to center stage. Supercrip proceeds to address the audience.)

SUPERCRIP: Seventh grade. The kids were terrible, the teachers... Like Ms. B before, were all terrible, the whole damn system was... Fucking terrible... Oh you are probably still wondering... Why didn't Cormac just turn into... (Pause and makes a flexing pose.) me?

(Pauses... Looks at Cormac. Talking directly to the image but he is gearing the response for the audience.)

SUPERCRIP: Good question... I don't really understand him, I guess he really wanted to be normal (17), even if it meant getting his ass beat daily.

(He runs his hands through his hair, puffing up his chest with a sigh of frustration.)

SUPERCRIP: I mean. Why not just turn into this mass of humanity you are feasting your eyes on right now?

(Double thumbs to his chest, still looking at Cormac reeling on the floor.)

SUPERCRIP: I guess changing into me seemed like the surest way for him to become abnormal. (18) Even though, he knew he could easily turn into me... He wanted to act like he was...

(Pauses with a questioning tone.)

SUPERCRIP: NORMAL?

(Laughs looking at Cormac, hovering on the floor in the fetal position, blocking the imaginary kicks from the 7th grade imaginary bullies.

Supercrip walks toward him.)

SUPERCRIP: You know... It wasn't anger that allowed me to "come out (19)".He was committed to never switching from (Disgusted.) that...

(Pointing at Cormac.)

SUPERCRIP: To Supercrip! (Double thumbs to himself.) No.... Changing would have been the opposite of normal to him. I think he wanted to be anonymous or maybe he was passing? (20) Yeah, that sounds more like it.

(Supercrip walks to the center of the stage.)

SUPERCRIP: They would never let him pass for normal... If you ask me, wanting to be normal is where all this garbage started from.

(Lights go down to pause for a second to allow Supercrip to exit stage right and reposition chairs. Lights then come back up. Six Chairs are now positioned in two rows of three facing the audience. Cormac is seated in his middle chair in the center back row. To the upper right, front of the stage, is an oval shaped object that looks like a mirror frame without a mirror. It is positioned with the faux reflection from left to right, not front to back. Off stage there is a girl's voice. It is Jen, she is the girl whom Cormac has a crush on and who he spends his lunchtime.)

JEN: "Hey Cory, I'm sorry I can't stay in and eat with you today. Mmm... I Gotta go... K... Bye!"

(Cormac yells to the voice off stage from his seated position.)

CORMAC: (Yelling) Nah it's cool, I'm good. No worries! (Transition from normal tone, and now sounds a little defeated.) You go ahead.

(Turns to the audience.)

CORMAC: She usually has lunch with me. Especially Thursdays. We Have these dumb pop quizzes after lunch. She and I always cram before the bell. Teacher never gets us... Lately though... (Mimicking.). She's Been too fucking busy!

(He gets up, and walks to the back of the right of the stage near the curtain. He acts like he is looking out a 'window', but there is no actual window, Cormac will mimic moving a curtain and looking out to his right where the voice came from, talking through the window to Jen even though she's not there.)

CORMAC: Yup... She's been busy...Really Busy! She tried to be slick, but I Know she is going out with that dickhead LJ.

(Looks back at the audience and then back out the window.)

CORMAC: You're asking yourself, "why don't I go outside with the rest of the "normals"? (21)

(Walks back to his seat and sits, but keeps a death gaze on the audience.)

CORMAC: Fuckin' Normals! The world revolves around you. Doesn't it? And poor suckers like me... We live our lives looking like... This!

(Stands up from the chair, and he pushes the rows to the sides, he uses enough force to "fly" the chairs in separate directions.)

CORMAC: I don't want to stay in this classroom any longer! But... (Takes a long pause.) I know what's out there... I know it's safer in here. (Assured tone.) And I don't have to deal with all that Bull Shit. (22) Jen knows that it's safer in here for me... She always knows everything... Except... How horny LJ is... Geez! She doesn't think I have the same piping!(23)

(The long oval-shaped frame serves as a mirror faux reflection. There is no actual mirror only a frame. It is located at the upper right front stage. It is positioned left to right so that Cormac can walk to one side and Supercrip walks to the other side and the audience can see them facing each other. Cormac approaches the mirror, Supercrip walks up, enter stage right, to serve as his reflection in the oval frame. As Cormac (On the left.) moves so does Supercrip (On the right.), Supercrip will mirror Cormac's movement.

CORMAC: I don't have to stay this way (Lifts arms up and down.) ... I could just switch (Spins around.) ... I could turn into him (Jumps.) ... With just a blink of an eye (Raises right hand and snaps his fingers.) ... Then (Stroking His face.) ... Then she will know I'm no different from those guys in fact... I'm better!

(Cormac tips mirror over... Supercrip fades to the back off stage, spotlight only on Cormac.)

CORMAC: So tired of this... So sick of this... That's it... Enough. You wanta monster... You got a monster. (24)

(Lights go out. Cormac exits stage left and Supercrip enters stage right. Lights come back on. Supercrip is right, rear of the stage, he motions to the same window, to move the faux curtains away, pauses as Supercrip views outside at Jen... Turns His head to the audience and smiles.)

SUPERCRIP: (Yelling.) It's Showtime!

(Lights fade out. Off stage, we hear incomprehensible roars of fear and agony from others to include Jen and LJ.)

END SCENE III

<u>ACT II</u>

Cormac is remanded to an institution. He has spent the remainder of his school age in places like these.

Initially, he was placed there by the court (25) because of the outburst with Jen and LJ in the seventh grade many years ago. Since then, he has never left the institutional setting. The stage is set with a bed frame, against the left side of the stage. A chair is facing the stage. The bed is part of his room (cell) where he is now residing. Lights go up and Supercrip is lying in bed.

<u>Scene I: The Institution</u>

Supercrip is laying with his hands behind his head, resting and looking at the ceiling, his feet are facing the audience and his head is to the rear of the stage. The bed is situated to the left front of the stage. The chair is placed to the right side of the bed at the front of the stage and is located within the confines of the area that is meant to serve as his room/cell.

Lights come on and Supercrip sits up to address the audience.

SUPERCRIP: Oh hi. You're still with me? Poor Cormac. Huh? It didn't take them long. Once they saw what he... I mean... I could do. They locked us both up in here in a.... A disability gulag! (26)

(Looks around and then back at the audience again.)

SUPERCRIP: Lovely, isn't it?

(Gets out of the bed and walks over to the chair situated at the right side of the bed, 'he is still within the confines of his stage cell', sits down, and he starts talking to the audience.)

SUPERCRIP: I don't know why Cormac gets all twisted up in knots about all of this?... Literally. I mean if you could be a superhero... Wouldn't you? It makes no sense to me... Just being stubborn. He insists on doing things the hard way... Ah... I'll let him explain.

(*Lights go out, Supercrip exits stage right in the darkness. Cormac enter stage left and lays down on the bed. Lights Come back on.*)

CORMAC: (Talking to himself.) I'm so stupid. (Sits up.) Why do I always let my emotions get the best of me? I can't let him talk me into doing shit anymore. (Frustrated tone.) I have people scared of me... They were more than happy to lock me away.

(*Lights lower, only a spotlight on Cormac, he arises from the bed and walks to the edge of the stage to address the audience.*)

CORMAC: Don't lie I know what you are wondering, "why don't you stay as Supercrip?" Well... Because... It's not who I am... Even if I think I am the hero; they will always see me as the villain (27). They've been doing this to disabled people throughout all of history. They get scared, they want me locked away from society. Thrown in a hole and never to be seen again! (28)

(*Cormac walks to the upper front-left stage; across the stage from him, Supercrip enters stage right in the dark. Spotlight is already on Cormac but now a second spotlight is ready to shine on Supercrip as they stand across from each other left and right.*)

CORMAC: This is so frickin lame! Society needs to have its villains along with its heroes. In fact, I'd venture to say there are more villains than heroes if you ask me. They all look like him!

(Cormac points across the stage and the second spotlight shines on Supercrip. Supercrip is standing acknowledging what Cormac is saying by nodding his head and makes a cheesy smile.)

CORMAC: I tried to avoid becoming him... But I still have these stigmas (29) placed on me... Why should I try and keep him contained?

(Stops to catch his breath. On the side Supercrip is motioning to Cormac to take it easy by showing his palms to him and moving them up and down to signify Cormac needing to relax.)

CORMAC: Because I knew this is where I would end up. Society makes monsters out of us when they can't explain us. (30)

(Supercrip is smiling, hamming it up and posing for the audience.)

CORMAC: Back then (Points to an empty space behind him.) Before all of this... I was harmless. I was Tiny Tim and one of those kids you see on the MDA telethon. (31)

(Cormac's hands brushing his hair back and with a tired tone. Supercrip acts like he is playing violin while Cormac speaks to the audience.)

CORMAC: Sometimes I miss being Tiny Tim... I miss being able to be...Non-threatening... Normal... Not stigmatized as a monster!

(Supercrip makes a prowling gesture with his hands toward the audience. Lights out.)

END SCENE I

Scene II: The Break Out

Lights come back up. Back in Cormac's room/cell. In the room/cell is Cormac's bed and a single chair facing the audience; It is the same way it was situated in scene 1. Supercrip is lying in bed, head to rear of the stage, and his feet toward the audience. Supercrip has hands behind his head staring upward and he appears to be talking to the ceiling, but he is actually addressing the audience.

SUPERCRIP: I really despise his weakness. Why does he care so much about what they think? They are never going to accept him. (Supercrip sits up and looks at the audience.) You see, this is where his problems stem from... (Exhausted tone.) He wants so damn bad to be considered "normal." He is willing to "pass" on who he is in order to be accepted. (32)

(Supercrip leaps out of bed and begins to walk past the room to the center stage, as he approaches center stage, the lights go low on the room and the spotlight focuses on Supercrip. Spotlight stays on Supercrip. Cormac enters stage left in the dark, he walks to the chair and sits down facing the audience.)

SUPERCRIP: Look at him.

(Second spotlight shines on Cormac seated.)

SUPERCRIP: Now look at me! Look at how awesome I am? Who on earth would want to be him? (Bragging tone) I'm what you call an ideal prototype (33).

(Spotlight goes out on Cormac. Turns the chair, back to stage)

SUPERCRIP: Now now now... Don't get me wrong. I don't despise him because he's a cripple. (Laughs to himself.) I despise him because he believes all that Bull Shit... He brought into the lie... The stigma of being less human... Less of a person... He let them obliterate his self-esteem (34).

(Lights out.)

SUPERCRIP: That was until that day...

(Supercrip exits stage right in the dark. Lights get turned on and Cormac is still sitting in his chair in his cell. Cormac is sitting with his back facing to the audience, but now he has a remote in his hand. He looks out into the audience as if it were the television screen. He lifts it to change the channels; voices from off stage are providing the sounds from TV.)

TV: What if I told you there was a way you could grow your hair back with...

(Cormac lifts the remote and gestures like he is clicking channels and he lifts his arm up when he makes the motion to change a channel.)

TV: This week on Dancing like a Star we are...

(Cormac gestures again to change the channel.)

TV: On Celebrity edition Quizzer all benefits go to the disabled children of America...

CORMAC: Jesus... There is only garbage on. *(Cormac gestures to get ready to change the channel but stops when he hears breaking news.)*

TV: Breaking news... We interrupt this program to bring you a special news bulletin. The hunger strike is going into its second week without any sign of letting up. The talks with the protesters have just come to a standstill. Wait... I think we have a couple of the protestors available for comment. (35)

(Cormac turns his head and looks to the audience and then looks back to the Television.)

TV: (Voices of Interviewee) "We see ourselves as consumers, as survivors as... Ex-patients! This is a coalition of disabled activist who want a seat at the table (36)."

(Cormac looks back at the audience, keeps gaze on them.)

CORMAC: (To the audience) And at this point...
My life had changed.

TV: "Basically institutionalism is incarceration...
No More Cells... No more Institutions... No More
Cells!"

*(Cormac Gets out of his chair and stares into the
audience.)*

CORMAC: (Quietly at first repeats the words to
himself.) No More Cells... No more Institutions...
No More Cells.

(Then he gets a little louder.)

CORMAC: No More Cells... No more
Institutions... No More Cells!

*(Then again, but this time he yells at the top of his
voice.)*

CORMAC: No More Cells!... No more
Institutions!... No More Cells!

(Voice of Institution Aide/Guard off stage.)

AIDE: Hey... Keep it down.

CORMAC: No More Cells!... No more
Institutions!... No More Cells!

AIDE: Hey Crip... I said Keep it down.

CORMAC: No More Cells!... No more Institutions!... No More Cells!

AIDE: That does it. You brought this on yourself crip.

(Lights go out. Cormac exits stage left as Supercrip enters stage right in the dark. Lights come back on with only Supercrip on the stage front and center...laughing as he yells at the audience.)

SUPERCRIP: No More Cells... No more Institutions... No More Cells! (Giggle) No More Cells... No more Institutions... No More Cells! Come and get me!

(Lights go off, sound of tussle in the darkness.)

SUPERCRIP: No More Cells... No more Institutions... No More Cells.

(Lights still down, sound of cell door closing.)
SUPERCRIP: No More Cells... No more Institutions... No More Cells.

END SCENE II

<u>SCENE III: GENETICS LAB</u>

Cormac has broken out of the institution and joined up with a protest group. He is planning to destroy a genetics lab that he deems is trying to commit genocide by eliminating impaired DNA for unborn children. Situated Center stage is a knee-high stand serving as the control panel for the genetics lab. Hazard Alarm is ringing. Lights Are flashing on and off, slowly. Then they go off completely. Overhead voice is heard.

LOUDSPEAKER: This is not a drill... This is not a drill... Evacuate... Evacuate...

(Cormac enters stage left in the dark. He walks over to the stand. Spotlight then shines on Cormac in front of the stands with his back turned to the audience.)

LOUDSPEAKER: This is not a drill... I repeat, this is not a drill... Evacuate...Evacuate... All parties... Evacuate.

CORMAC: (To himself.) Keep cool... Don't panic.

(Lights out. Enter Supercrip stage right. An explosion is heard, lights come back up. Cormac has not moved but now Supercrip appears stage right, standing on the edge of the stage looking at the audience.)

SUPERCRIP: He did it? (Astonished.) Wow? Can you believe it?

(Looking at the crowd.)

SUPERCRIP: Oh you're wondering what he did? Well, he stopped a massacre. 'Ne a genocide! (37)... Confused? Ok let's rewind.

(Supercrip walks to the center stage, and the spotlight follows him. He points his finger up to the sky and says.)

SUPERCRIP: Eugenics!(38) Or let me put it in another more common phrase. How about... (Points finger above his head again.) Discrimination!

(Looks at the audience... Assumes they still don't understand.)

SUPERCRIP: Ok so you're not familiar with it?... Try and stay with me.

(Points into the audience.)

SUPERCRIP: Hey, you there. (Picks out a random audience member) Yeah you.

(Speaks directly to the audience member he picked out.)

SUPERCRIP: See how your head is odd shaped. Yeah! ... I'm talking to you. That's due to bad breeding...

Your mama and daddy didn't match. (39)

(Laughing to himself... He points again to the crowd.)

SUPERCRIP: And you.

(Pointing to another random person in the audience.)

SUPERCRIP: Well... It's your skin color... How can I put this? It's too... (Emphasizes the word dark) Dark! You'd really be perfect if you had less melatonin my friend... No worries, not your fault... And Him.

(Points to his left, spotlight goes to Cormac in front of the stand that is serving as the genetics lab control panel.)

SUPERCRIP: Geez... where do I start? You see all the things wrong with him? Don't you? Yuck right? It's all a matter of genetics. We can thank a guy named Quetelet.(40) Don't worry if you don't remember his name, let's call him 'Ol Man Q. He gave us this concept of "normal" and Cormac just doesn't fit in... 'Ol Man Q would have called him... (Thumbs Down.) Abnormal!

(He walks over to Cormac. Cormac appears lifeless; his shoulders are slumped down and his back is still facing the audience. Supercrip starts to manipulate the lifeless Cormac. He picks up Cormac's limp arm and then lets it drop, and he then tips Cormac and Cormac

starts to wobble and Cormac loses but clumsily regains his balance. Supercrip walks around Cormac, who continues to stand with his back to the audience. Supercrip is looking him up and down the same way someone would look at a used car.

He talks to the audience while looking at them over Cormac's shoulder.)

SUPERCRIP: Yup, he is a defective(41) like 'Ol Man Q would say. Q's work gave rise to the (Trumpy voice impersonation, with air quotes.)"Beautiful" philosophy called Eugenics... If we only paid attention, it would be the perfection of the species... The proof that natural selection exists!... Man... (Shaking Cormac's limp shoulders with a sigh of disgust for Cormac's body.) I'd really like to trade this in!

(Supercrip pushes Cormac out of the spotlight... Second spotlight follows Supercrip as he starts to walk away from Cormac. Supercrip walks to the right front of the stage. Cormac returns to his position, back faced to the audience, and the first spotlight continues on Cormac.)

SUPERCRIP: You all recall we "left" prison?... Oh I mean (Uses air quotes to describe the word.) the "institution". Cormac was inspired by the courage of others... He saw the work being done to create his view... Our view...Using our lens... You know...The disability lens!(42)

(Supercrip throws his fist in the air.)

SUPERCRIP: But we had one looming issue... It was a force we couldn't overcome... (Sarcastically over- dramatized tone) Stigma!(43)

(Supercrip shakes his fist to animate how it was a foiled effort, as he looks toward the audience.)

SUPERCRIP: Try as we might. The laws like ADA, IDEA, the 504(44) changed the rules... But they did not change the world enough. The view of being broken...Being non-abled... Being less than human.

Gave rise to these damn genetic labs.(45)

(Supercrip starts to walk to the left side of the stage. The spotlight remains on Cormac standing over the stand with his back still to the audience.)

SUPERCRIP: It wasn't bad enough to live with the stigma that we were all broken(46)... Now there is an all-out assault!... (Pause.) It's a deliberate effort to end anything that resembles him. (Points to Cormac.)

(Supercrip regains his composure, sits on the edge of the left stage to address the audience.)

SUPERCRIP: How does it feel to have a future? I mean to know you can be...(Annoyed Tone.) Anything you want to be? How does it feel to grow up without a target on your back?

(Sitting on the edge of the stage, Supercrip looks up to the sky, as he prepares to address a higher being.)

SUPERCRIP: (Looking Up.) Explain to me, why them? Why do they get the free pass? They don't know the "joy" of having someone trying to eradicate them from the face of the earth to improve it!(47)

(Looks back down, and then at the audience again.)

SUPERCRIP: How do they plan to improve it?...You ask?... By genetically altering the future of course... So in the future there won't be any more Cormac's... Is that ok with you?

(Supercrip pointing to the audience asking the question.)

SUPERCRIP: Is it? (Shrugging.)... I mean c'mon... You left us no choice.

(Light fades out on Supercrip sitting in the dark. Only Cormac continues with his spotlight. He turns around so the audience can see his face.)

CORMAC: Ok, deed is done. Come and get me. *(Lights out. Voice from off stage.)*

POLICE: Down on the ground! Down on the ground! Don't Move... What the hell happened here? You... Down on the ground!

(END SCENE III)

<u>ACT III</u>

The genetics lab was destroyed by Cormac. The incendiary devices he used caused multiple injuries to staff to include a few fatalities that resulted from the bomb blast. The scene brings Cormac back to the courtroom.

Cormac and Supercrip have completed explaining their history and actions to the court. Cormac is once again awaiting sentence.

Scene I: <u>**BACK IN THE COURTROOM**</u>

Stage lights come on. Cormac on the left, is standing next to Supercrip on the right with two feet in-between them. They are standing behind the folded table and chair. Cormac has his head down, while Supercrip is looking out into the audience. Then Cormac looks up and Supercrip looks down. Spotlight fades from Supercrip to shine only on Cormac.

CORMAC: Your honor.

(Cormac looks down, Supercrip looks up. Supercrip snaps his fingers. Supercrip looks down, and Cormac looks up again.)

CORMAC: You now have the use of your voice and can move again...Ok?... Good.

(Voice of Judge from off-stage.)

JUDGE: So glad you are going to let us do our job, you are in a lot of trouble Mr. Cormac.

CORMAC: I apologize your honor, for that outburst, and I apologize to the jury.

(Supercrip looks up smiles and then lowers head again).

JUDGE: I'm going to regret this, but in light of all the theatrics... do you have any last words before sentencing.

(Cormac looks to Supercrip on his right. Lights are lowered with spotlight only on Cormac.

Supercrip gives him a pushing gesture as if he is encouraging him to move. Cormac steps forward, maneuvers around the chair and walks up to the edge of the folding table...Pauses... Cormac's head is down and does not look up.)

JUDGE: Well Mr. Cormac if you have nothi...

(Stopping the judge mid-sentence.)

CORMAC: I do.

JUDGE: You do, do you? Let's hear it?

(Cormac Looks up at the audience.)

CORMAC: I do... I do not accept this!... I do not think you are able to see what I see. You think you and I are vastly different but in actuality... We are one in the same. Your honor?... You honor beauty! That's what you fuckin honor. You honor your definition of normal and beauty! You are like Dorian Gray(48)...

But what you see... When you see me... Is someone to pity, and I am someone that validates your own sense of being beautiful...Being aesthetic. (49) But what is beautiful? What is grotesque?...What you see is what you honor... Is it what you actually see? It's all a God Damn façade. It's gonna all go away!

(Slams his hand on the table.)

CORMAC: You are all such hypocrites. You want me to stay this way to allow you to have your superiority... Admit it!

(Off Stage.)

JUDGE: Mr. Cormac... This tirade is about to end.

(Cormac looks at the voice... stares... takes a second.)

CORMAC: Why are you really trying to lock me away?... Aren't you actually just trying to exile abnormality? Erase me from your sight?

JUDGE: Its' called Justice Mr. Cormac!

CORMAC: Ok let's talk about Justice... Let's do that... I'm gonna substitute your word for mine. You don't want justice... You want normalcy... You yearn for the normate world... I exist... And I am evidence that your normal is Bull Shit... If I'm OK... then your ideas are not OK. You worship Bull Shit. If I'm alright... Then you're All Wrong!.... When you see me, it makes you nervous. (50)

(Cormac snaps his fingers and the lights go down, Cormac exit stage left. Supercrip has

moved up to where Cormac was standing on stage in front of the table. Lights go back up.)

SUPERCRIP: Here is your justice (Grabs his crotch.) ... I could burn this building to the ground with a glance... I could wave my hands and this entire courtroom becomes a mass casualty event... If you are normal...Then I am superior and guess what? ... You are the defectives now!

(Pauses...laughs.)

SUPERCRIP: Welcome to the Defective Community. You remember don't you... The same asshole defective excuse you used for rampant slavery, for legalized sterilization, for vilifying immigrants. (51)

(Points finger to the air.)

SUPERCRIP: If I am superior to you... If I have powers you don't... Aren't you in fact... The defectives?... Shouldn't we be trying to eliminate you?(Pause.) I knew it... I fucking knew it... This would never work... These views... These stigmas (52) are not based on science... They are based on your BS aesthetic need to make your world normal... And they are all hard baked in you!

(He stops and looks at the audience and says.)

SUPERCRIP: (Inquiry.) You want justice for only you?...That does it...Right?

(Supercrip raises his hands to the air, shaking them vigorously as if to conjure a lightning bolt from the air. He maintains his eye contact with the audience as he's doing this; never breaking his stare at them during the motion.

Lights begin to flash on and off with a sound like roaring thunder off stage.)

SUPERCRIP: Staring bother you?...(53) Prepare for death normals... Prepare for... Justice!

(Flashing stops after a few seconds then lights off. There is silence for a second, Supercrip exits stage right and Cormac enters stage left in the darkness. Cormac returns to the table and sits down in the chair facing the audience. Lights On.)

CORMAC: Well, your honor... I've said my peace... And I think I made my point. (Off stage Supercrip is heard laughing.) Oh yeah... One last thing... At anytime, anyplace, anywhere... I can always switch into him... But don't worry, I choose not to... Why?

Because this is who I am... And I want you to know you can't change me. You'll never be able to change me.

(Looks Down, stands up...then looks out into the audience.)

CORMAC: But you (Pause.)... It's up to you. Change is up to you.

(Lights Out.)

END

END NOTES AND CITATIONS:

1. Ref Imbecile: "You want him you take him. I'll give him to you. I can't do any more than I've done." Brother of the character labeled as the "Imbecile" in the book Blood Meridian (McCarthy, 1985, p. 268).

2. Ref Obesity: IAW the Food and Drug Administration a Body Mass Index of 30 kg/m^2 or more is considered obese (Food and Drug Administration, 2022).

3. Ref Communication-Related Disabilities: "These remain deeply stigmatized. Disability rights advocates are acutely aware of the possibility that some voters will mistakenly equate difficulty speaking with difficulty thinking (Astor, 2022)."

4. Ref Normate: "Intentional use of dual narrators to present themselves as disabled and superior human beings. She (Garland-Thomson) argues that the normate can assume authority and wield power because of their bodily configuration and cultural capital (Meekosha, 2009, p. 63)."

5. Ref Disability/Incarceration Connection: "Connecting analysis of incarceration with disability, is also a call to pay attention

to the lives of mostly poor people of color

who are incarcerated worldwide in nursing

homes, institutions for those with labels of mental illness and/or intellectual/developmental disabilities and prisons (Ben-Moshe, 2013, p. 113)."

6. Ref Breaking the Fourth Wall: "When you're watching movies or TV, there is a wall that separates the audience from what's happening on the screen. (Called) the imaginary "fourth wall." When a character does this it is called Breaking the fourth wall (Nonnetwork, LLC, 2022)."

7. Ref Summer of 2003 Protest: six people gathered at a small building in Pasadena, California and starved themselves for twenty- two days (Lewis, 2013).

8. Ref Disabilities Rights Laws: "Fundamental change implied by the assessment of disabled persons as a minority group, however, is the rigorous enforcement of anti-discrimination laws. The provision of the Education of All Handicapped Children Act of 1975, and Section 504 of the Rehabilitation Act of 1973, which prohibits discrimination against disabled persons in programs receiving federal financial assistance, have never been conscientiously implemented" (Hahn, 1987, p. 21)."

9. Ref Isolation: "Disabled are isolated not because of social dynamics, e.g., the stigma associated with disability or systematic prejudice, but instead because of their own individual moral or emotional defects (Raphael, 2012, p. 78)."

10. Ref Orientalism: "America's glorification of independence has not served disabled people well; argument: American glorification of Independence doesn't help the disabled - goal is to be self-sufficient and not a drain. Depending on others for Help not the American Way (Linton, 1998, p. 3)."

11. Ref Media Portrayal: "In the media, poverty, as with disability, is something to be overcome. ...rarely if ever portrayed as systematic problems; rather they are routinely seen as individual ones (Davis, 2017, p. 43)."

12. Ref Disabled Media Representation: "Meanwhile, representations of people with disabilities in television, film, literature, and the arts needs more detailed investigation. It seems probable that an analysis of not only the monster, criminal, and maladjusted characterizations, but also other types, would reveal a hierarchy of disability, involving a complex interaction among such factors as visibility, severity, mode of functioning, and proximity to the face and head (Longmore, 2003, p. 146)."

13. Ref Metaphor: "Disability pervades literary narrative, first, as a stock feature of characterization and, second, as an opportunistic metaphorical device (Snyder, 2013, p. 222)."

14. Ref Exceptional: "Exceptionality group as a group sharing specific abilities or disabilities that valued or that require special accommodation within a given microculture. Thus, a person may be identified as exceptional in one ethnic group (or other microculture defined by gender, social class, religion, etc.) but not in another (Johnson, 2006, p. 11)."

15. Ref Childs Perspective Special Education: "Special education is looked upon by our youth to mean that you are dumb, you have less value, you do not belong (Conway, 2005, p. 3)."

16. Ref Labeling: Because special education often separates children with disabilities from their non-disabled peers, whether physically or nominally, it can also promote the very stereotypes of freakishness, pity, and lack of ability from which people with disabilities struggle to be free (Conway, 2005, p. 6)."

17. Ref Normalcy: "Not simply trying to include disability under the rubric of Normal but to question the idea of normality, and to expand the definition of disability into such concepts as

neurodiversity, debility and capacity, chronic illness, invisible conditions, and the like (Davis, Reader, The Disability Studies, 2013)."

18. Ref Abnormality: "Disability is a broad term in which cluster ideological categories as varied as sick, deformed, ugly, old, crazy, maimed, afflicted, abnormal. or debilitated-all of which disadvantage people marginalizing by devaluing bodies that do not conform to cultural standards (Garland-Thomson, 2002, pp. 74- 75)."

19. Ref Coming Out: "Coming out is primarily portrayed as the process of revealing or explaining one's disability to others, rather than as an act of self-acceptance facilitated by a disability community (Samuels, 2013, p. 320)."

20. Ref Passing: "By passing as non-disabled, by minimizing the significance of their impairments within their own personal and social lives . . . people with hidden impairments often make an effort to avoid the perceived stigma attached to a disabled identity (Samuels, 2013, p.321)."

21. Ref Normal Imagery: "Garland Thomson's work on imagery and the disabled body is one such example. She uses the concept of the 'normate' for those who can present themselves as definitive or superior human beings. She argues that the normate can assume authority and wield power because of

their bodily configuration and cultural capital (Meekosha, 2009, p. 63)."

22. Ref Social Isolation: "Perspective of some disability studies scholars, a "special" education can be equated with segregation, social isolation, and stigma (Conway, 2005, p. 3)."

23. Ref Sexuality: "As a child, Ashley (sterilized disabled infant) has no need of reproductive organs; as a disabled person, she has no sexuality (Kafer, 2013, p. 57)."

24. Ref Monster Stigma: "Stigmatized trait assumedly taints every aspect of the person, pervasively spoiling social identity. That "spread effect" is evident... the notion of loss of humanity, the idea that disability results in loss of self-control. The disabled character thus endangers the rest of society. The dangerous disabled person is not necessarily a criminal or a malevolent monster but may be a tragic victim of fate (Longmore, 2003, p. 135)."

25. Ref Incarceration: "Analyzing imprisonment from a disability studies lens also necessitates a closer look at the social and economic conditions of disablement and incarceration rather than looking at disability as a cause for criminal acts (Ben-Moshe, 2013, p. 134)."

26. Ref Disability gulag: the labeled warehouse for disabled people that is often called "the institution (Ben- Moshe, 2013, p. 132)."

27. Ref Monstrous Historical Depiction: "Historical figure of the monster, as well, invokes disability, often to serve racism and sexism... monster originally described people with congenital impairments (Garland-Thomson, 2013, p. 338)."

28. Ref Societal Bad Guy: "bad as having a physical disability—a hunched back, a hook, wooden leg, an eye- patch, an "ugly" face, or an animal-like monstrous appearance. Indeed, classic "bad guys" including pirates and witches are often generated. In contrast, "good" is often portrayed as individuals with long flowing hair and a smiling face, something akin to a stereotypic angel (Bejoian, 2014, p. 5)."

29. Ref: Stigma: "Stigma stems from differences. By focusing on differences, we actively create stigmas because any attribute or difference is potentially stigmatizable (Brown, 2013, p. 150)."

30. Ref Disabled Hierarchy: It seems probable that an analysis of not only the monster, criminal, and maladjusted characterizations, but also other types, would reveal a hierarchy of disability, involving a complex interaction among such factors as visibility, severity, mode of functioning, and proximity to the face and head (Longmore, 2013, p. 28)."

31. Ref Pity: "Tiny Tim - A Christmas Carol. Tiny Tim was more than a character in Dickens's tale. He was a ubiquitous cultural figure... Tim's image was made into a constant and powerful cultural symbol (Longmore, 2013, p. 34)."

32. Ref Pass: "Attempting to "pass" and derogating others like themselves are two ways in which stigmatized people effectively accept the society's negative perceptions of their stigma (Brown, 2013, p. 154)."

33. Ref Ideal Prototype: "Ideal prototype (e.g., young, white, tall, married, male, with a recent record in sports) that Stafford cites may actually possess traits that would be the source of much scorn and derision in another social context (Brown, 2013, p. 149)."

34. Ref Self-Esteem: "People with low self-esteem are more likely to identify and maintain negative stereotypes about members of stigmatized groups, such people are more negative in general (Brown, 2013, p. 152)."

35. Ref Disabled Protest: "summer of 2003, six people gathered at a small building in Pasadena, California and starved themselves for twenty-two days (Lewis, 2013, p. 115)".

36. Ref Disabled Representation: "Mad Pride members mark this shifting epistemology by referring to themselves as consumer/Survivor/ex-patient's groups. This hyphenated designation, usually shortened to c/s/x or 'consumer/survivors,' highlights that today's Mad Pride is a coalition of critical activists—some of whom have a more radical epistemological critique than others (Lewis, 2013, p. 121)."

37. Ref Extermination: "Historical tradition which has included the widespread practice of genocide as well as the extermination of one million disabled persons in Nazi Germany (Hahn, 1987, p. 20)."

38. Ref Eugenics: "The reason has something to do with the economy of visual storytelling in an ableist culture. This in turn comes out of the legacy of eugenics and the current hegemony of ableism itself (Davis, 2017, p. 44)."

39. Ref Human Improvement: "Eugenics movement's greatest proponent, defined the movement as "the science of the improvement of the human race by better breeding (Dolmage, 2011, p. 27)."

40. Ref Quetelet's average man: "Quetelet's average man was a combination of both a physically average and a morally average construct (Davis, 2013, p. 16)."

41. Ref Defective: "eugenics became obsessed with the elimination of "defectives," Popular school of thought, eugenics arose as a way to eliminate defectives and deviants (Davis, 2013, p. 17)."

42. Ref Disability Lens: "The purpose of developing a disability lens is to bring attention to what is already there across our existing curriculum, inviting students to be aware of the ambivalent, often contradictory ways that cinema's concern for issues of ability—along with other markers of identity such as race and gender—has been used in our imagining of the body (Raphael, 2012, p. 84)."

43. Ref Abnormal: "Often, attributes or behaviors that might otherwise be considered 'abnormal' or stigmatized are labeled as 'eccentric' among persons of power or influence (Brown, 2013, p. 149)."

44. Ref ADA Regulation: "The ADA protects against discrimination on the basis of 'disability,' so a plaintiff has to qualify as having a disability to bring a claim under the statute. ADA protects against discrimination on the basis of 'disability,' so a plaintiff has to qualify as having a disability to bring a claim under the statute (Emens, 2013, p. 211)."

45. Ref Genetic Screening: "The debate over genetic screening, other words, necessarily includes the voices of those who do not believe that it should be taking place, or who believe that it should take

place but that it should not be morally binding or dispositive when it comes into conflict with moral absolutes (Barube, 2013,p. 108)."

46. Ref Broken Body: "provokes the fear that the disabled body will reproduce another 'damaged' child—from a 'broken' body and a 'broken' home (Millett-Gallant, 2013, p. 401)."

47. Ref Flawed Body: "widespread selective abortion on the basis of prenatal diagnosis is the greatest insult: some of us are 'too flawed' in our very DNA to exist; we are unworthy of being born (Saxton, 2013, p. 98)."

48. Ref Dorian Gray: "On the one hand, bodies do not seem to matter to who we are. They contain or dress up the spirit, the soul, the mind, the self. I am, as Descartes explained, the thinking part. At best, the body is a vehicle, the means by which we convey who we are from place to place. At worst, the body is a fashion accessory. We are all playing at Dorian Gray, so confident that the self can be freed from the dead weight of the body, but we have forgotten somehow to read to the end of the novel. On the other hand, modern culture feels the urgent need to perfect the body (Siebers, 2013, p. 278)."

49. Ref Aesthetic: "General definitions of the word Aesthetic refer us to the 'branch of philosophy dealing with the study of aesthetic values such as the

beautified and the sublime,' the 'study of the rules and principles of art,' and, most notably in relation to visually impaired embodiment (Bolt, 2013, p. 95)."

50. Ref Aesthetic Nervousness: "Aesthetic Nervousness is seen when the dominant protocols of representation within the literary text (Quayson, 2013, p. 202)."

51. Ref Immigration: "One of the fundamental imperatives in the initial formation of American immigration policy at the end of the nineteenth century was the exclusion of disabled people 'the undesirable immigrant' (Baynton, 2013, p. 26)."

52. Ref Dehumanization: "Goffman states a stigmatized person is constituted through interaction as the 'not quite human person'...produced through a special relation between 'attribute and stereotype,' takes three major forms... to "blemishes of character"; 'tribal' factors (e.g., race, nation, religion); and through 'abominations of the body' Person with disabilities suffers from stigma of dehumanizing (Titchkosky, 2015, pp. 5-7)."

53. Ref Staring: "Disabled people have variously been objects of awe, scorn, terror, delight, inspiration, pity, laughter, or fascination-but they

have always been stared at (Garland-Thomson, 2002, p. 56)."

SUPERCRIP REFERENCES:

ASTOR, M. (2022, OCTOBER 26). How People With Disabilities Saw Fetterman's Debate Performance. New York Times.

Barube, M. (2013). Disability, Democracy, and the New Genetics. In L. J. Davis, The Disabilities Reader (pp. 101-114). New York: Routledge.

Baynton, D. C. (2013). Disability and the Justification of Inequality in American History. In L. J. Davis, Disability Studies Reader (pp. 16-33). New York: Routledge.

Bejoian, D. C. (2014). Cripping School Curricula: 20 Ways to Re-Teach Disability. The Review of Disability Studies, 3-13.

Ben-Moshe, L. (2013). "The Institution Yet to Come": Analyzing Incarceration Through a Disability Lens. In L.

J. Davis, The Disabilities Reader (pp. 132-143). New York: Routledge.

Bolt, D. (2013). Aesthetic Blindness: Symbolism, Realism, and Reality. Mosaic: An Inter-disciplinary Critical Journal, 93-108.

Brown, L. C. (2013). Stigma: An Enigma Demystified. In L.

J. Davis, The Disabilities Reader (pp.147-160). New York City: Routledge.

Conway, M. A. (2005). Introduction: Disability Studies Meets Special Education. The Review of Disability Studies: An International Journal, 3-9.

Davis, L. J. (2013). Reader, The Disability Studies. (Fourth, Ed.) New York, NY: Routledge.

Davis, L. J. (2017). The Ghettoization of Disability: Paradoxes of Visibility and Invisibility in Cinema. In H.

B. Anne Waldschmidt, Culture – Theory – Disability: Encounters between Disability Studies and Cultural Studies (pp. 30-49). Germany: Bielefeld transcript Verlag.

Dolmage, J. (2011). The Rhetorical Construction of Disability and Race at Ellis Island. Cultural Critique , Vol. 77 (Winter), 24-69.

Emens, E. F. (2013). Disabling Attitudes: U.S. Disability Law and the ADA Amendments. In L. J. Davis, The Disabilities Reader (pp. 205-233). New York City: Routledge.

Weight-Loss and Weight-Management Devices. Retrieved from FDA.GOV: https://www.fda.gov/medical-devices/products-and- medical procedures/weight-loss-and-weight-management- devices.

Garland-Thomson, R. (2002). The Politics of Staring: Visual Rhetorics of Disability in Popular Photography.

T. Snyder, Disability Studies: Enabling the Humanities (pp. 56-75). New York: Modern Language Association of America.

Garland-Thomson, R. (2013). Integrating Disability, Transforming Feminist Theory. In L. J. Davis, The Disability Studies Reader (pp. 333-353). New York City: Routledge.

Hahn, H. (1987). Civil Rights FOR Disabled Americans: The Foundation of a Political Agenda. Farsta: Independent Living Institute.

Johnson, J. R. (2006). Validation and Affirmation of Disability and Deaf Culture: A Content Analysis of

Introductory Textbooks to Special Education and Exceptionality. Review of Disability Studies An International Journal, 3-32.

Kafer, A. (2013). Feminist, Queer, Crip. Bloomington: Indiana University Press.

Lewis, B. (2013). A Mad Fight: Psychiatry and Disability Activism. In L. J. Davis, The Disabilities Reader (pp.

115-131). New York: Routledge.

Linton, S. (1998). Claiming Disabilities. New York: New York University Press.

Longmore, P. K. (2003). Screening Stereotypes: Images of Disabled People in Television and Motion Pictures. In P.

K. Longmore, Why I Burned My Book, and other essays on disability (pp. 131-146). Philadelphia: Temple University Press.

✳

LONGMORE, P. K. (2013). Heaven's Special Child. In L. J. Davis, The Disability Studies Reader (pp. 34-41). New York: Routledge.

McCarthy, C. (1985). Blood Meridian or The Evening Redness In the West. New York: Vintage Books.

Meekosha, H. A. (2009). What's So Critical About Critical Disability Studies? Australian Journal of Human Rights, 15.

Millett-Gallant, A. (2013). Sculpting Body Ideals: Alison Lapper Pregnant and the Public Display of Disability. In

L. J. Davis, The Disabilities Reader (pp. 398-410). New York: Routledge.

Nonnetwork, LLC. (2022). Definition and Examples in Film & TV. Retrieved fromnofilmschool.com: https://nofilmschool.com/breaking-fourth-wall-definition-meaning and-examples.

Quayson, A. (2013). Aesthetic Nervousness. In L. J. Davis, The Disability Studies Reader (pp. 208-219). New York: Routledge.

Raphael, R. (2012). Teaching Film and Disability Studies. In L. F. Petro, Teaching Film (Options for Teaching) (pp. 74-86). Modern Language Association.

Samuels, E. (2013). My Body, My Closet: Invisible Disability and the Limits of Coming Out. In L. J. Davis, The Disabilities Reader (pp. 316-332). New York City: Routledge.

Saxton, M. (2013). Disability Rights and Selective Abortion. In L. J. Davis, The Disabilities Reader(pp. 87- 99). New York: Routledge.31.

Siebers, T. (2013). Disability and the Theory of Complex Embodiment—For Identity Politics in a New Register. In L. J. Davis, The Disability Studies Reader (pp. 278-297). New York City: Routledge.

Snyder, D. M. (2013). Narrative Prosthesis. In L. J. Davis, The Disabilities Studies Reader (pp. 222-235). New York: Routledge.

Titchkosky, t. (2015). Life with Dead Metaphors Impairment Rhetoric in Social Justice Praxis,9.1. Journal of Literary & Cultural Disability Studies.

COMPENDIUM TO
THE TRIAL OF SUPERCRIP
AND THE CONVICTION OF
NARRATIVE PROTHESIS

COMPENDIUM: INTRODUCTION

In "The Trial of Supercrip (And the Conviction of Narrative Prosthesis)," I attempted to explore disability, identity, and societal tropes. Through the story of Cormac and Supercrip, readers are invited to consider the ways in which societal norms and expectations shape our understanding of ourselves and others. The play challenges readers to question their assumptions and to see the world through a different lens.

The story of Cormac and Supercrip is one that is both thought-provoking and emotionally engaging. As readers follow the journey of these two characters, they are confronted with complex issues related to disability, identity, and beliefs. The play encourages readers to think critically about these issues, to question their own assumptions, and to see the world in a new way.

However, the exploration of these themes should not end with the play. In the compendium of essays that follows, I will attempt to dive deeper into the concepts that were either presented directly or touched upon in the play, with the intent to provide additional context and issues that impact people with disabilities. Through a series of deliberately written essays, I would like to invite readers to continue their exploration of the multifaceted issues impacting people with disabilities and gain further insight into the drama that enveloped Cormac and Supercrip.

The essays will cover a wide range of topics, from the societal tropes used as a narrative for disabled people to the concept of the "disabilities lens." Each essay provides a unique perspective on the themes explored in the play, allowing readers to gain a deeper understanding of the complex issues at hand. As readers move from the play into the compendium of essays, it is hoped that it would spark their curiosity if they never had it or reignite it if they have not thought about it in a while. They are encouraged to explore further the terms and concepts presented in the compendium, including those presented in "The Trial of Supercrip (And the Conviction of Narrative Prosthesis)." Through this intentional combination of dramaturgy and focused essays, the goal is to present a contemplative and provocative exploration of disability, identity, and societal norms that will leave the readers engaged and interested in the field of disability studies.

COMPENDIUM: DISABILITIES EXPERIENCE

(Being a caregiver to an intellectually disabled (ID) older brother shaped my identity in Compendium: Disabilities Experience. I offer how I managed my brother's health, finances, and safety throughout his life, facing societal stares and potential threats. Society's portrayal of disability as "un-normal" and undesirable, as discussed in Leonard Davis's essay "Introduction: Normality, Power, and Culture," heightens the fear for his safety and guilt and defensiveness as "the other child." Discrimination and mistreatment of individuals with disabilities reflect my feelings of insecurity as a sibling to someone with ID as well as concern for his well-being.)

MY PERSPECTIVE IS THAT of a sibling to a mentally disabled older brother. He is 59, and mentally he is closer to the age of 8 years old. If you can picture the image of an 8-year-old boy holding the hand of his 18-year-old brother, you would assume the traditional roles of older and younger brothers are being displayed. Yet in my case, the roles of caregiver and oversight are switched, and that young boy is the one looking out for the older sibling. This is the life I have led, and probably something that may look adorable on the outside looking in, but internally as "the other child" you build an identity based on the care of your sibling. Fast forward forty years and that dynamic of hand holding has expanded to health care, managing his finances, crisis like emergency dental surgery and constantly looking out for his safety in the age of COVID where shaking hands with strangers can become and life-endangering affair. I am afraid for his personal safety, fear for his emotional state, and fear of external "stares" as Raphael mentioned[1] in his video presentation. There is tremendous guilt as a sibling of someone with a disability, and to my shame, there is also a heightened defensiveness. As the other child, you feel a need to assure those who stare are either 1: not staring at you or 2: know that if they continue to stare, they are going to be putting themselves in jeopardy because your base and original role of protector is activated when staring at your sibling occurs.

Perhaps the roots of my fear for his safety and concern for my image could be attributed to what we have been unwarily conditioned as the medical concept of disability. Where the idea of "un-normal" are illustrated by Leonard Davis in his essay "Introduction: Normality, Power and culture" he states, "On the other hand, as sufficient research has shown, more often than not villains tend to be physically abnormal: scarred, deformed, or mutilated." This view displays the disabled as being un-normal, unsavory, unappealing, and worst of all unwanted in society. Rounding back to my paranoia of fear, and my constant concern that someone will take this as a license for cruelty and in some cases superiority. That same person would not only stare but possibly attack him either verbally or physically. I retain this fear, albeit rational or not, it worries me because it has been my reality more times than I care to remember.

I look forward to opening my horizons when it comes to discovering the abilities of the disabled. Hopefully it will allow me to let my guard down and relax my fears as I learn more about my brother's untapped strengths and what he can provide to society as a full functioning disabled man.

COMPENDIUM: CRUELTY AND DISABILITIES

*(In COMPENDIUM: CRUELTY AND DISABILITIES, the
fears that were addressed in the previous essay are further
explored. As with Cormac in his experience while in school, this
theme of bullying is addressed. However, in this essay, a very
familiar culprit plays the role of the bully)*

A MEMORY CAME TO MIND after writing,
"COMPENDIUM: DISABILITIES AND EXPERIENCE",
it was of the 2016 presidential election and then candidate
Donald Trump mocking a reporter from the New York Times
(CNN, 2015). In doing so he used bodily gestures that
mimicked someone with impaired motor control.

I questioned, "how can anyone be so cruel?" Pushing
politics aside, I contemplated what would give someone a
license to behave this way? Regarding the article,
"Introduction: Normality, Power, and Culture" by Lennard J.
Davis, he offers for anyone to understand the disabled body,
one must return to the concept of the norm; the normal body
(Davis, 2013).

Was this the rationale for cruelty? Due to the lack of a
visible normal body, did it provide the license to abandon
applying standards for decent human behavior? I utilized this
reading to explore the recesses of those who would take license
to be cruel and contrasted it with what my current bias has
been conditioned regarding the criteria for normalcy. As a
former military member, I recalled the standards provided in
AFI 1-1 that stated:

All Air Force members must maintain a high standard of dress and personal appearance. This standard consists of five elements: neatness, cleanliness, safety, uniformity, and military image.

(USAF, 2023)

In the military, failure to meet standards is punishable by disciplinary actions, and conceivably there are those who may hold these types of standards for everyone including those who are disabled. Furthermore, it is not a far supposition to assume those who hold extreme rigor for standards, have difficulty tolerating anyone who fails to meet their view of normality.

Unfortunately, that answer is too convenient for me. I believe the answer dwells within in macro cultural conditioning of what is normal, approved, and standard. I considered what Davis wrote about Quetelet and his concept of "errors", and how he provided standards that could be equally applied to the distribution of human features (Davis, 2013). Quetelet's argument is that normal humans have normal human distributed features, and conversely those who have un-normal distributed human features (ie those who have a "defective" body) appear inhuman. It starts to tread into dangerous territory where the argument can lead to a belief that having a body that is abnormal is defective. Davis provides, "When we think of bodies, in a society where the concept of the norm is operative, then people with disabilities will be thought of as deviants" (Davis, 2013).

Perhaps the license to be cruel is rooted in what Davis refers to as the "defective class". Like failing to meet the standards in the military, Quetelet's standard for normalcy could be applied to anyone with an abnormal body as "the habitual criminal, the professional tramp, the tuberculous, the insane, the mentally defective, the alcoholic, the diseased from birth or from excess... the formulation "defective class" (Davis, 2013).

The benefit of having the field of Disabilities Studies, pries open the bias, concealment, and inaccurate imagery much of the community experiences regarding concepts of normal, standard, defective and deviant. With more insight provided by, the field, possibly my inquiry into the nature of cruelty will get a more satisfying answer.

COMPENDIUM: LITERATURE AND DISABILITIES

(In COMPENDIUM: LITERATURE AND CAPABILITIES, I was not able to find the satisfying answer I sought from the previous essay. The theme of cruelty became more prevalent with my decision to choose Blood Meridian and Cormac McCarthy's use of the character he called the "imbecile". The use of a narrative prosthesis by way of exploiting a character with intellectual disabilities for shock value brought all the salient points home and encouraged me to write the Trial of Supercrip)

I READ BLOOD MERIDIAN by Cormac McCarthy (McCarthy, 1985) before entering into the world of Disabilities Studies. It is considered a tenet of Western canon by many literary scholars. I concur the imagery, the violence, and the untethered historic view leave a long-standing impression. However, I have issue with its adoration. Unnecessarily, it employed a minor character as a disabled man whom McCarthy referred to as the idiot and the imbecile (McCarthy, 1985). Bordering on the edge of sadism and pointless cruelty, he subjected the character to treatment that involved horrific instances of abuse without any attempt at a literary resolution that could explain its purpose in the story.

My ire with McCarthy became granular with further reading into the field of Disabilities Studies. The readings were dense with multiple areas to explore, however, the concept of condoned cruelty continued to resonate with me. The "license" I wrote about in "COMPENDIUM: CRUELTY AND DISABILITIES" regarding the CNN reporter who was mocked about his disabilities, was further illuminated in "What's So "Critical" about Critical Disability Studies?" by Helen Meekosha and Russel Shuttleworth. These authors introduced the concept of "orientalism" as a device in film and literature utilized to romanticize the "normate" western ideal hero (Shuttleworth, 2009). The authors point out the work of Rosemary Garland Thomson's imagery and the disabled body, where she provides the concept of the "normate" being capable of becoming a superior human (Shuttleworth, 2009). Conversely, I took this to mean those with a disabled body are not capable of being superior humans if this logic is applied equally.

It offers a bleak view of the world for McCarthy's imbecile, and I presume it provides McCarthy with literal justification to disregard the "imbecile's" humanism in his character portrayed in Blood Meridian. In the reading Claiming Disabilties by Simi Linton, the author explains how a character like the imbecile could be tolerated. Linton states:

> "...the loathing of society or maybe an unchecked impulse spurred by an internalized self-loathing. It is likely that often the reasons entail an admixture of any of these various parts (Linton, 1998)."

My interpretation of McCarthy's overt callousness in his depiction of the imbecile fills a void that desires to loathe anything that pales to measure up to the idea of Orientalism. Perhaps there is a fear, if not for fate of chance, he (McCarthy) too would be the imbecile. Employing cruel tactics ensures those who register with orientalism avoid questions like these Linton inquires:

> "Are you saying my life is not worth living, that I should not have been born, that I don't have a place in your version of the world (Linton, 1998)?"

Fortunately, there are those who believe disabled lives are worth living, they have a rightful place in the world, and they have given rise to the "social model." In The Social Model of Disability by Tom Shakespere, he stipulates the social model offers a way to distinguish allies and enemies, identify social barriers, improve the esteem of disabled people, and build a collective identity (Shakespere, 2013). He goes on to caution against the social model becoming a barrier to further progress because it has the potential to alienate the medical community and take on characteristics of radicalization. However, had there been better advocacy prior to the release of Blood Meridian in 1985, perhaps McCarthy's imbecile would lay waste on the writer's room floor with other malevolent bad ideas in literary history.

COMPENDIUM: ISOLATION AND DISABILITIES
(In COMPENDIUM: ISOLATION AND DISABILITIES, I steered away from the consuming concept of cruelty and turned my attention toward the idea of isolation. Similar to what Cormac in "Trial of Supercrip" endured as a child at home and in school, these feelings of isolation and loneliness were eventually the triggers that allowed him to succumb to Supercrip)

REGARDING THE CONCEPT of isolation, it was a challenge to find an obvious connecting thread to the past compendium passages on cruelty and identity. I thankfully came across a reference from earlier in my career. In an article, I noticed a reference to "Bowling Alone" by Robert Putnam (Putnam, 2000) and it brought back memories of heated debates with co-workers regarding the concept of social capital and the numerous interpretations we had related to it in our grant peer reviews at the Hawaii Community Foundation. Over twenty years ago he wrote about the phenomenon of social structural decline. I was introduced to it as part of our required staff readings. My first impression of it was as high-brow utopian fodder. My attitude surmised it as something you wasted your coffee breaks talking about because I never believed it could be applied.

I left that career with crafted skepticism in hand, and until now, I never thought of Putnam again. Astonished, I may have been wrong about social capital and the power of Putnam. In the article, "Deaf Studies in the 21st Century Deaf Gain and the Future of Human Diversity" by Murray and Bauman, the concept of social capital was resurrected. I recalled my criticism was it focused too much on anecdotes and I felt it never provided any practical means to achieve social capital or fortify against social isolation. Conversely, Murray and Bauman countered my thoughts through navigating a path for social capital to become actionable. They did this through there discussion of the "Deaf walk". By employing the "Deaf walk" to a larger cultural audience it could have lessons for "an increasingly isolated society" (Murray, 2013).

With luck or either cosmic serendipity, social capital has gotten a new lease, and it is my connective tissue for this week. At face value, there are too many varieties to thread together a comparative mosaic, but if you step back, I imagine these readings all share a need for community advocacy and awareness. For instance, in "Centering Justice on Dependency and Recovering Freedom" by Eva Feder Kittay she states:

> *"It is not the necessity and neediness of dependency that repels us, it is the disadvantages that are a consequence of political, social, and economic social arrangements."*

(Kittay, 2015)

She counters the stigma that dependency evokes negativity, and her advocacy takes issue with the belief that dependency creates social ills like Putnam's isolation. Her essay outlines the complexity of social arrangements in her use of the concepts of "inevitable dependency" and the "inextricable interdependence" of humans (Kittay, 2015). Putnam's antithesis was social isolation, and one could derive Kittay fears that same fate for her daughter Zoe who is permanently dependent on someone else for her care. Her attempt to change the dynamic of dependency helps to underscore the point Putnam made all those years ago about the danger of social isolation.

The need to assist society in viewing disabled support, dependent caregiving, and adhering to inextricable interdependency became the crossroads where these readings met. Activities like the Deaf walk as a practice of Social Capital has the potential to become a productive metaphor like a "social crosswalk". A salient application of a social crosswalk is presented in "The Unexceptional Schizophrenic: A Post-Postmodern Introduction" by Catherine Prendergast (Prendergast, 2013). Rather than provide an explanation for the stigma of schizophrenia, she provides a perspective that embraced it as something you live with and not a neurological malady. She offered the work of Ken Steele who founded "New York City Voices" primarily as a journal to inform about legislative issues but writing the journal itself served its own enfranchising purposes" (Prendergast, 2013). Though Steele has since passed away, the testimonies of New York City Voices are still robust and thanks to social media and the internet, the audience is worldwide (Voices, 2022) .

I hold to the belief two decades running; the theory of social capital on its merit alone cannot provide what it presumes. However, when used as an additive to other more tactile social engagements, it has the potential to become a value-added community-building asset that prepares us to use the social crosswalk more responsibly and joyfully.

COMPENDIUM: BECKETT AND DISABILITIES

(In COMPENDIUM: BECKETT AND DISABILITIES, I gained inspiration from another literary icon, Samuel Beckett. This came to mind after reading the work Prendergast had done as well as the life work contributed by Steele with City Voices. Beckett's play Waiting for Godot is thought to be a staple of the Theater of the Absurd, and it also provides a glimpse into the psyche of mental illness portrayed in various ways by the characters in the play. The dialogue between Estragon and Vladimar provided insight into the development of the dialogue in the Trial of Supercrip.)

EXCERPT FROM "WAITING for Godot" by Samuel Beckett

>**Vladimar: He wants us to help him get up.**
>**Estragon: Then why don't we? What are we waiting for?**
>**Vladimar: We must hold him? Feeling Better?**
>**Pozzo: Who are you?**
>**Vladimar: Do you not recognize us?**
>**Pozzo: I am blind. (pause)**
>**Estragon: Perhaps he can see into the future?**

(Beckett, 1954)

OVER THE YEARS I HAVE developed a wish list (bucket list is probably the more appropriate term) of books I have wanted to read in my life. One of them was "Waiting for Godot" by Samuel Beckett. I cannot lie, I've picked it up and put it down many times, just because I could not grasp "what the heck" was going on. The story is completely non-linear for my strident and structured military DNA. Yet as we found out in our readings this week, Beckett and a list of other Nobel qualified writers used devices like, "narrative prothesis" and "aesthetic nervousness" in their work. Sure enough, I reached back to the bookshelf for Beckett, and I was able to connect the pieces, and suddenly it was not as confusing as I remembered it being in the past.

For instance, in Aesthetic Nervousness by Ato Quayson, he provides "the idea that the disabled body is somehow a cipher of metaphysical or divine significance (Quayson, 2013)." This explains the purpose behind Beckett's sudden, for no evident reason, making the character Pozzo become blind. It is not a stretch to consider he used narrative prosthesis with the blinding of Pozzo. In Narrative Prothesis by David Mitchell and Sharon Snyder, it seems Beckett borrows from "Sophocles attempt to self-blinding Oedipus to illustrate the corporeal relations of dramatic myth and disability (Snyder, 2013)."

Although now that I am aware he may have used these literary narrative devices, it did not help to navigate the chaotic dialogue in "Waiting for Godot". At times it felt like there were three different discussions all happening at once, but then I recalled Beckett was referred to in the "The Unexceptional Schizophrenic: A Post-Postmodern Introduction" by Catherine Predergast. Amazingly the clues started to reveal themselves regarding Becketts intention to be absurd.

She wrote:

"John Cage and Samuel Beckett, neither of whom were diagnosed schizophrenics. Cage and Beckett quickly, however, become metaphors of schizophrenia through Jameson's analysis. In the end Jameson leaves us with an aestheticization of the schizophrenic experience (Prendergast, 2013)."

With these newly acquired tools, I moved "Waiting for Godot" from the "I'll never understand this" to the "OK, I think I get it now" column. I must admit, figuring out Beckett may have been worth the wait.

COMPENDIUM: GENERATION X AND DISABILITIES

(In COMPENDIUM: GENERATION X AND DISABILITIES, the passage reflects a personal and intellectual journey of growth, understanding, and a commitment to critically examine and challenge preconceptions about disability and its role in society. Using metaphor, I accept that with age, knowledge can be acquired, and with that a better appreciation and understanding of disability. Which leads me to ask a generationally influenced question, ""why do marginalized groups need to emphasize the hardships of the past rather than solve the problems of today?")

RECENTLY I HAVE HAD the feeling of someone walking into a garage and magically realizing they actually know how to properly use a tool that had been lying dormant, unused and collecting rust for years. As someone who lived all the cliché phases of generation X, I had some dread about returning to school in the "modern time". However, I felt I needed to find truth, and not rely on the information fed by cable news or social media. Unfortunately, I realized from my time in the military, you can effectively convince yourself of anything, right or wrong, if you are motivated enough to win an argument. One of those arguments was, ***why do marginalized groups need to emphasize the hardships of the past rather than solve the problems of today?*** I included the disabled as part of the marginalized groups. Even though I now have disabilities according to the VA, I care for someone who has disabilities, and I probably worked with others who hid their disabilities; I was woefully ignorant of the significance of what it meant to be disabled.

In "What's So Critical About Critical Disability Studies?" by Helen Meekosha and Russel Shuttleworth, I objectively read for the first time about the infamous Critical Race Theory that I have seen numerous times vilified in the political arena. I learned it has roots with the Frankfurt Theorist, and it harkens back to the desire to utilize critical thinking (Meekosha, 2009).

Furthermore, Critical Disabilities Studies exist as an offshoot of the work started by the Frankfurt Theorist long ago, and it is something that is necessary for many of the same reasons Critical Race Theory is needed. Had I not started on this journey, I would not understand the value of critical (skeptical) curriculum and why marginalized communities need them for advocacy and legitimacy.

This lack of critical thinking and avoidance of the rigors of skepticism are the breeding grounds for stigmas like the ones encounter by the disabled. As Linton provided, able bodied members of society assume in western cultures a disability will always be a stigma for the individual to cope with (Linton, 1998). The conventional acceptance of the stigma associated with having to 'live with it' was questioned in articles that present disabilities as assets, exemplified in 'Deaf Studies in the 21st Century: Deaf Gain and the Future of Human Diversity' by H-Dirksen L. Bauman and Joseph J. Murray. They argued "the validation of sign language revolutionized the study of language, so too must the nature of literature be reconsidered (Murray, 2013)."

So, I will attempt to answer my own question: "why do marginalized groups need to emphasize the hardships of the past rather than solve the problems of today?" I must emphasize it is an evolving answer, but I found some of the solution provided by Rosemarie Garland-Thompson in "The Politics of Staring: Visual Rhetorics of Disability in Popular Photograph (Garland-Thomson, 2002)." The hardship is rooted deep in history, they are wrapped around social injustice, barriers for inclusion, and overt misinformation. To ignore the hardship, may also be fueling the stigma. The end state could be as Thompson puts it "a move toward the process of dismantling the institutional, attitudinal, legislative, economic, and architectural barriers that keep people with disabilities from full participation in society (Garland-Thomson, 2002)." Looking to the past, enables us to look toward the future. Doing it honestly and with efficacy are benefits of the CRT and Disabilities Studies, sharpening old tools for use again.

COMPENDIUM: RED CARS AND DISABILITIES

(In COMPENDIUM: RED CARS AND DISABILITIES, the passage explores the author's growing awareness of the portrayal of disabilities in literature and media, emphasizing the repetitive nature of certain tropes and their impact on how disabilities are perceived in storytelling. It applies the Baader-Meinhof Phenomenon, to illustrate how bias can occur.)

THERE IS A COMFORTABLE feeling you have when you live in ignorant bliss. You drink from the garden hose of life, not knowing there is lead in the pipe. You drink the shoyu base in the BBQ chicken, before the chicken is cooked. You watch television your entire life without awareness of the blatant cliches and pandering at the expense of marginalized groups. Particularly in the case of those with disabilities, you never think twice of the tropes airing on Disney+ and Netflix. Until you do. I googled a question, "what do you call something you never notice, then suddenly, you only notice it? he "red car syndrome" came up. It has an academic

The background, known as the "Baader-Meinhof Phenomenon" (Pacific Standard Staff, 2013; Placeholder1). Essentially, when you see a red car on the road, you may have a propensity to continue seeing red cars. This reminded me of "Compendium Literature and Disabilities" when I mentioned the "imbecile" that Cormac McCarthy wrote about in "Blood Meridian." In the book the imbecile is caged like an animal, led on a leash and covered in his own filth (McCarthy, 1985). He grunts and groans because he was not written in the narrative with the capacity for speech. I was perplexed where the literary value was in making this character. I recently learned the term, "narrative prothesis," and its use in literature and film narratives have become more and more abundant to me. I realize McCarthy needed the disabled character to add depth to the story, he could not care any less for the depiction or accuracy of the disability because it was his means to an end. Now that I can see how it is used in far too many tropes; it has become my "Red Car."

I experienced the Baader-Meinhof Phenomenon once again in "Why Disability Identity Matters: From Dramaturgy to Casting in John Belluso's Pyretown" by Carrie Sandahl. The term that she introduced etched in my memory now is, "cripping up." She provides "casting non-disabled actors as disabled characters is called pejoratively cripping up, referencing the outdated practice of white actors "blacking up" to play African American characters (Sandahl, 2008)." Here again, like the use of narrative prothesis by McCarthy, the use of the device of cripping up, is another Red Car I can't stop seeing. It's everywhere, in movies like X-Men, Avatar, and I am Sam.

Baader-Meinhof Phenomenon of disabled tropes in narratives reveals itself like an epidemic; it would be impossible to try and ignore. The Autistic Victim: Of Mice and Men and Flowers for Algernon by Sonya Freeman Loftis provides two cases of cognitive disabled men, where their disabilities are crucial to the flow of the stories. (Loftis, 2015) They each have tragic ends, but the tragedy is tied into the fact their disabilities are harbingers of their difficulties. In Lennie's case he is "euthanized" and in Charlie's case he reverts to the cognitive void. I've read these stories early in my youth, seen variations of them on film, and never had I thought about the use of disabilities as narrative trope. Until I did, and now this is all I can see.

COMPENDIUM: SPECTACLE AND DISABILITIES

(In COMPENDIUM: SPECTACLE AND DISABILITIES, the passage introduces the idea of disabled representation in professional wrestling, highlighting the absence of disabled characters in villainous roles and raising questions about the reasons behind this choice. It encourages readers to reconsider wrestling through the lens of disability, offering a new perspective on the sport.)

MY MOM LOVES TO WATCH professional wrestling, she struggles with the names, and often changes her allegiance after weekly viewing, but it is something she does religiously without fail. In turn, I have found a fondness in watching, somewhat for nostalgic reasons, but mostly because it provides an opportunity for her and me to enjoy something sports related... sort of.

Wrestling is a spectacle, and it revives the concept of the freakshow that Raphael Raphael writes about in his essay, "Teaching Films and Disability Studies". Where the concept of the freakshow was "a mode of spectatorship privileging body spectacle, the freakshow was influential on the emerging form of film, particularly the cinema of attraction (Raphael, 2012)." It is absolute low-brow entertainment, there are some underpinnings that wreak misogyny, racism, cultural appropriation, and colonialism. It is all unfolded on the table for the public to partake; some secretly taking it with shame.

However, it provides an extreme example of what the public desires in its spectatorship and it could be considered the modern day freakshow with one exception. The freaks in this freakshow are able bodied wrestlers, and rarely are the disabled portrayed in any characters in the lineup. Compared to what has been practiced in film, this is not the case. Longmore provides, "giving disabilities to villainous characters reflects and reinforces, albeit in exaggerated fashion, three common prejudices against handicapped people: disability is a punishment for evil; disabled people are embittered by their "fate"; disabled people resent the nondisabled and would, if they could, destroy them (Longmore, 2003)."

In wrestling you have hulking, enraged, and spite driven characters that play the villain, and they are considered the "heal". Placing a disabled person in this role, perhaps would be a bridge too far for viewers to accept. Yet in the mode of spectatorship, we have witnessed in history disabled people placed in the role of the heal. For example, "Sophocles later moves to Oedipus's self-blinding as a further example of how the physical body provides a corporeal correlative to the ability of dramatic myth to bridge personal and public symbology (Snyder, 2013)."

So why are no disabled characters playing the heal in wrestling? If it flies in the face of what has been common practice and used as narrative prothesis in almost every James Bond movie, what keeps the script writers in professional wrestling in bounds with disabled representation? Could it be, in this world the valued characters are the heals, and they must align with our able-bodied concept of "normate" where Thompson provided, "the normate can assume authority and wield power because of their bodily configuration and cultural capital (Meekosha, 2009)." In this light strangely enough, there is a case for disabled people being discriminated against because they are not allowed play the heal. In this perspective, like with everything else, wrestling has taken on a whole new perspective when we apply the disabilities lens.

COMPENDIUM: HUMOR AND DISABILITIES

(In COMPENDIUM: HUMOR AND DISABILITIES, the passage raises questions about the nature of humor, particularly in the context of disability, and evaluates the impact of the Farrelly Brothers' approach in disrupting traditional narratives surrounding disability in mainstream media. I argue for the acceptance of disability without the need for it to signify or be resolved in storytelling, challenging prevailing ableist cultural norms.)

It was a particularly terrible day, a car bomb exploded outside of the gate. They suffered many casualties, to include some dead-on arrival. It's been especially gruesome in the ER where they have been piling up bodies left and right for hours. With no breaks, the ER Staff has been feverously working on the wounded. One medic, takes a step back and looks at the attending ER Physician:

Medic: Sir, this is the fifth person on the floor to die after the attack!

ER Doc: That's terrible. My God this must be the record for fatalities since the war started. What do you think? It's a record huh?

Medic: Ah no. Doc there were like 10! And that was last month before we got here.

ER Doc: Hmmm...hey what time is it?

Medic: Why?

ER Doc: Cmon, tell me what time is it?

Medic: Sir, it's 11:30PM?

ER Doc: Awesome, we still have 30 minutes left!

I hope I don't need to explain the punchline. The point behind this dark joke is to illustrate the use of humor. Is it funny? Probably not for a disabilities class, but for someone who may have PTSD and worked in actual trauma, it may be the type of thing that gave them enough energy till the end of their shift. Gallows humor, albeit in poor taste, can give respite during some uncomfortable and inhumane situations. Having the ability to laugh at yourself and others in situations most humans don't experience may give them permission to feel human. This question of is it funny, can also be asked is it honest? Is it true, is it uncomfortable, is it relieving, is it sad. Those are all criteria you can add to the prime question of whether it is funny or not.

Perhaps a better question to ask is, "is it lame?" I watched the Ringer, and the first thing I noticed was this was not a Farrlley Brothers directed or written movie. They were producers. This explained why it was a terribly made movie, to include the non-disabled acting, flat script, and lack of resolution in the end (what was the bet again?). The use of the mentally and physically disabled actors was not the most distressing part. The floundering of a unique opportunity to showcase mentally disabled actors in a better movie is the unforgivable thing. It was lacking anything laugh out loud funny except for the ice-cream line, when they athletes returned back to camp after sneaking out to watch the movie, "When the F!$K did we get ice cream!" (Blaustein, 2005) That was funny because it was an honest reaction I could picture occurring after the athletes had been promised something and it was not delivered. Here I laughed at the actor's reaction, that was compounded by the "freedom" the actor had to say what he wanted because his disability removes those social barriers for him. That was funny.

I argue that this wasn't a real Farrlley brothers movie, but I do give it credit for mirroring one aspect of the Farrlleys, the Ringer did not try and resolve the disabilities of the athletes. They were allowed to be themselves, and this is something the Farrelly's have been striving for in the movies that I would consider they actually made. Le Besco quotes Norden in his article that "mainstream society is profoundly uneasy with Others and usually tries to neutralize them in one of two ways: cure them or get rid of them (LeBesco, 2004)." The Farrlley's are given credit for not doing this in their movies, and this practice carried over to the Ringer.

Siebers claims that "the political unconscious upholds a delicious ideal of social perfection by insisting that any public body be flawless. It also displaces manifestations of disability from collective consciousness ... through concealment, cosmetic action, motivated forgetting, and rituals of sympathy and pity (LeBesco, 2004)." When we think about the work of the Farrlley's we have to give them credit for disrupting Seibers philosophy and essentially going for the joke regardless of the able or disabled identification by the audience. But is it funny? I must ask, "did you laugh?"

What the Farrlley's have done counters what Davis wrote about the public acceptance of disability. He states, "they will wonder why the normalcy of the film is being tampered with. In an ableist culture disability cannot just be – it has to mean something. It has to signify, public can not cope with disability just happening, there has to be a reason (Davis, 2017)." Yet, for the Ringer it just did, and for the Farrelly brothers I hope it continue to exist for all their movies without excuse. Ideally, the answer to the question, "is it funny?" will be, "Yes, it is because it is!"

COMPENDIUM: REPRESENTATION AND DISABILITIES

(In COMPENDIUM: REPRESENTATION AND DISABILITIES, the passage highlights the potential harm in being overly strict and making absolute rules in the realm of art and expression. The fear is that this approach might miss out on the nuances and satire present in creative works, potentially resulting in a form of crudely essentialist thinking. It explores the nuanced nature of advocating for disability representation in the arts and media. Davis's question becomes a central point, prompting consideration of the potential consequences of mandating rules for disabled-only involvement in creative projects.)

"SO, IF I SAY THAT ONLY disabled actors can play disabled parts, am I in effect saying that only some people should be accommodated? (Davis, The Ghettoization of Disability: Paradoxes of Visibility and Invisibility in Cinema, 2017)"

Davis poses this question and I consider it the crux of a provocative issue. He introduced the term, "crudely essentialist" (Davis, 2017), and it caused me to ponder at what point are we straying from enriching society with inclusiveness or becoming the force that sets up boundaries and constraints. Davis provides the phenomena of becoming crudely essentialist as double edged, where he realizes that if he is to attempt to force the issue of setting rules that require disabled only involvement, he also provides a yard where only they can reside and exist. It effectively becomes a way to inhibit equality for all because it galvanizes the concept of what I consider "owned otherness" for disabled. Nuance and dynamic thinking must come into play because this is not something that should be absolute like making a ruling on the level of benzine allowed in the public water table. Sadly, Davis's question does not provide a black and white answer in and of itself.

If we let the scenario play out, and the result of this effort becomes badly made films like the Ringer (Blaustein, 2005), what good will it do for mandate rules on behalf of the disabled? If the product that is fought for is below par, the impact will be a bomb and no willing investor is going to take a risk on the next project. The answer may not come from the industry or artists. The solution could exist with the consumers, the audience, and the marketplace. It is hard to ask the audience to accept the argument that movies with disabled people are worthwhile when they have the Ringer as their benchmark to compare.

Conversely, there are examples of projects that worked and spiked a demand and positive response from the viewing public. Take a show like Arrested Development, when Hollywood star Charlize Theron played the role of a mentally disabled woman. It employed a complex comedic story arc challenging the audience to consider who is really suffering, the disabled character or the non-disabled protagonist (Feig, 2005) It also challenges the audience to consider the conflict of morale vs immoral, and innocent vs guilty. Though the joke revolves around her being mentally disabled, the conflict is not based on her disability, rather the issue is a crisis of internal character. It illustrates that moral character does not become disabled with cognitive impairment.

There is a case to make that Charlize Theron's character was morally able and the Bluth family suffered from a moral disability. I will admit Arrested Development is guilty of utilizing the "star vehicle" Davis writes about (Davis, 2017). However, in all honesty, her star power is what makes the joke work in this instance. It's funny because the joke was written to be absurd and a satire on ableism and morality, which leads me to understand the harm in becoming draconian and making absolute rules when it comes to art and expression. For fear of missing out on the joke, being accurate could result in being crudely essentialist.

COMPENDIUM: NUANCE AND DISABILITIES

(In COMPENDIUM: NUANCE AND DISABILITIES, the passage highlights the complexities of issues related to disability, selective abortion, and advocacy for disabled actors. It suggests the importance of a nuanced approach that considers multiple perspectives and avoids overly simplistic or accusatory viewpoints).

LENNARD DAVIS WROTE about the phenomenon of being "crudely essentialist" occurring when advocates demand disabled roles be played only by disabled actors, and thus the effect of making a potential decision without taking the nuances of all possible factors involved into account (Davis, 2017). This stringent course of action may positively affect the advocacy of inclusion of disabled actors in film, but there is a cost of exclusion for those who are not disabled in the aftermath that needs to be considered in the nexus.

In "Disability Rights and Selective Abortion" by Marsha Saxton, this concern of crude essentialism became consonant with me. Her arguments against selective abortion, were dug in deeply to the point her rationales felt like they were based on pure conjecture absent of a qualified argument. For example, she takes a generous leap in the following statement, "It is clear that some medical professionals and public health officials are promoting prenatal diagnosis and abortion with the intention of eliminating categories of disabled people, people with Down's syndrome and my own disability, spina bifida, for example (Saxton, 2013)."

I may have some bias coming from the medical community, but I am curious to see where the foundation for the "elimination" claim comes from. The oath taken in medicine is "do no harm." The standard of practice in medicine is to first consider the wishes of the patient. It is the patient who makes the final decision on treatment. Her sentiment is the medical community has a hidden agenda to eradicate disabilities, and my experience is that good medicine has no hidden agenda. Do no Harm. There needs to be significant data to back her accusations, without it I had difficulty siding with the points she was attempting to make about selective abortion and prenatal screening being done out of convenience more than necessity.

Barube in contrast, takes on the issue of selective abortions like Saxton, however I think his approach was more effective. Rather than place a value statement on the motive of parents who chose to have selective abortion, he posed the following question, "it raises the question of what conditions we should screen for, and what we should do if and when we detect them....The larger question at stake, of course, is the question of who should inhabit the world, and on what terms (Barube, 2013)." Less accusatory, and perhaps its just a matter of style, but in his arguments he appeals to the consciousness of the parent. Ultimately putting the locus of control with them. It was a far more effective way to persuade a similar point of view.

COMPENDIUM: INSTITUTIONS AND DISABILITIES

(In COMPENDIUM: INSTITUTIONS AND DISABILITIES, the passage emphasizes the negative consequences of systemic isolation of disabled individuals, both in terms of societal attitudes and economic incentives, highlighting the need for more compassionate approaches.)

THESE READINGS SHARED common traits regarding the systemization of disabilities and how they are used to subjugate others. Lewis wrote about how hospitalization was used as a tactic to isolate the disabled from society, and Ben-Moshe added the layer of incarceration as a means to the same ends. The stigmatization that Lewis wrote is what gave rise to the Mad Pride movement. The disabled endured societies belief their disabilities were essentially personal tragedies, and it justified what he considered the "hegemony of disability (Lewis, 2013)." This gave society license to hideaway, lock-up and isolate the disabled, because their problems do not belong to society if you subscribe to this point of view.

Ben-Moshe in his article, "The Institution Yet to Come: Analyzing Incarceration Through a Disability Lens", provides an even lesser view of the purpose of systemic isolation of the disabled. He writes, "political economists of disability argue that disability supports a whole industry of professionals that keeps the economy afloat, such as service providers, case managers, medical professionals, health care specialists etc (Ben-Moshe, 2013)." Adding to many of the deficits that exist with the privatized prison system, Ben-Moshe provides another reason against the practice. The term we used in the military was the "self-licking ice-cream cone" or perhaps less obtuse description, the "perpetual motion machine." Unlike the argument that Lewis provided about how disabilities should be viewed as an individual problem because society is not responsible, Ben-Moshe illustrates, that society has a monetary benefit from systemically isolating disabled in their prisons and institutions. The commonality I found with both views was the welfare of the disabled far off in the distance, ignored and isolated.

COMPENDIUM: ELECTIONS AND DISABILITIES

(In COMPENDIUM: ELECTIONS AND DISABILITIES, the passage discusses the contentious race for the Pennsylvania Senate seat between Dr. Mehmet Oz, the Republican candidate, and Lieutenant Governor John Fetterman, the Democratic challenger. Fetterman, who recently experienced a stroke, disclosed his condition before a debate with Dr. Oz, and the author observes the deliberate use of disability rhetoric to discredit him.)

WE ARE TWO WEEKS AWAY until the mid-term elections, and one of the most contentious races is the race for Pennsylvania Senator recently vacated and sought by Dr. Memmeht Oz, a former talk show host, the Republican Senatorial Candidate, and the current Lieutenant Governor John Fetterman the Democratic challenger to the race. Fetterman has recently experienced a stroke that has caused him to have auditory lapses in his speech, this was self-disclosed by him in his introduction before his debate with

Dr. Oz. As ugly as these things can get, what makes this of interest to the lay political observer, and more so a student in Disabilities Studies, is the observation of deliberate disability rhetoric used to discredit someone. Ironically the one hurling the insults is a medical doctor.

In an article from the New York Times titled, "How People With Disabilities Saw Fetterman's Debate Performance" by Maggie Astor, she provides "One in four Americans has a disability, but disabled politicians are rarely on the national debate stage.... Fetterman's appearance (was) a powerful moment, but public reactions were painful (Astor, 2022)." She later goes on to provide perspectives of other disabled viewers who found his performance encouraging. Although, she harkens back to the bias Fetterman endured during the night and potentially nation-wide as this election has a considerable amount of importance in terms of the balance of power in the Senate. She stated, "Communication-related disabilities remain deeply stigmatized. Disability rights advocates are acutely aware of the possibility that some voters will mistakenly equate difficulty speaking with difficulty thinking (Astor, 2022)."

This speaks to Hahn's writing about "an atmosphere in which disabilities are commonly regarded as signs of weakness, helplessness, and biological inferiority (Hahn, 1987)." What Fetterman recently endured in the presidential debate, could be seen as a further illustration of the bias Hahn provides, but it also is in some ways an indication that the hard work of inclusiveness is in play. Having a stroke does not automatically signify someone is unable to participate in a debate. The same way that wheelchairs do not signify a loss of mobility. Pathways and access need to be provided to deter making them "inaccessible or blocked by architectural barriers (Hahn, 1987)."

The codifying of the "Education of All Handicapped Children Act of 1975, and Section 504 of the Rehabilitation Act of 1973, which prohibits discrimination against disabled persons in programs receiving federal financial assistance (Hahn, 1987)." It empowers disabled to consider engaging in types of activities they would have once been discriminated against. With that in mind, some may say that Fetterman lost the debate in whole but scored a moral victory for the disabled community. I believe the victory was more than moral because it sets a benchmark for anyone with disabilities to go where their ambition will take them (Ben-Moshe, 2013)

COMPENDIUM: MINORITIES AND DISABILITIES

(In COMPENDIUM: MINORITIES AND DISABILITIES, the passage provides a comprehensive exploration of the challenges faced by disabled individuals in various contexts, including historical isolation, political dynamics, and the complexities of inclusion and minority identity.)

EMENS PROVIDES SOME poignant questions on the issue of inclusion, "why would voluntary efforts to diversify an institution incorporate disability? Why would an institution choose to seek out people who would bring costs and no benefits? And how could a university have a Disability House that students— disabled and even nondisabled—would choose to join? They wouldn't (Emens, 2013)." These inquiries are pretty harsh, and the answer is sorrily true from my experience. Whether driven by profit, performance, or just pure power motives, altruistic actions on the part of the corporation, headquarters or main office normally are few and far in between. They require the hammer of law and the nail of compliance to make them behave like a good corporate citizen. There are far too many variables at play to ensure companies will abide to things like benzine levels in drinking water, sprinklers in high rises and ramps where the stairs start and end.

That said, I am confused with the logic Hahn provided in his article regarding the minority group model. The ADA law is tailored specifically to have organizations comply to the needs of disabled people; the specificity of this law works in the favor of disabled, they benefit by not being labeled as minorities in that sense. I do not understand where the sentiment that "antidiscrimination" is not something the disabled community can fully claim because they lack the designation of a minority group. Therefore, it is theorized if it did occur, disabled people would be positioned to enact "the eradication of bias and segregation requires extended efforts to secure equal rights for disabled citizens and the righteous enforcement of antidiscrimination measures (Hahn, 1987). I can side with the concern that disabled people feel they are missing out on the "privilege" of being a minority group. What I do not fathom is the belief that only those labeled as minority groups can have a bonafide claim of being discriminated against.

Speaking as a minority and someone who has experienced discrimination in the past because of it, if there were some ways to avoid going through it, I would have preferred the road with less suffering. Perhaps someone can help me better understand why it is favorable for disabled people to consider themselves as a minority? I'm not saying it is something that I devalue; I just have some difficulty buying the rationale that it makes life better when you are in the minority.

COMPENDIUM: SPECIAL EDUCATION AND DISABILITIES

(In COMPENDIUM: SPECIAL EDUCATION AND DISABILITIES the passage includes my reflection on my experience with a presume disability in a multicultural household, where higher education was not strongly encouraged, and how the system may have contributed to feelings of exclusion and "otherness." This personal narrative shed light on the intersectionality of race, socio-economic status, and disability which all culminated in shaping educational experiences and perceptions of self-worth.)

THROUGHOUT MY YOUTH I was placed in remedial classes, this was the normal practice for most of my elementary years. I can still recall my kindergarten teacher vehemently objecting to me being allowed to remain with my class. She was convinced I needed to be placed in special education. This was done not to meet my educational needs, but moreso as a tactic to have a "bad" kid removed from her class. Having had siblings there were cognitively disabled at the time, my father was dead set against this taking place. I had two brothers, one who passed away of brain cancer when I was 12 who was diagnosed as mentally retarded, and my oldest brother who has injured induced cerebral palsy and schizophrenia. Getting the news at that time, that a third son of his was needing placement in special education was more than my father could bare. Keep in mind, this is 1976, the work of Ed Roberts, Judith Heumann, and Justin Dart, had only a nascent start as the education system got accommodated to the "passage of key legislation and rules and regulations including the Rehabilitation Act of 1973, the Individuals with Disabilities Education Act (IDEA), and (eventually) the Americans with Disabilities Act (ADA) (Johnson, 2006)."

My father got his way, and I remained with my co-hort. Aside from being in a household where there was daily competition for attention and needs, it was reasonable to understand that I did not exactly have a head start when it came to education. In fact, having a learning disability was a normal attribute in my household because it seemed everyone had something "wrong" with them. I cannot speak to the mindset of my kindergarten teacher, but I do recall feeling her disdain for me. To this day I still can recall an incident when she threatened to physically hurt me, and I do not recall feeling any comfort or kindness from her the way I suspected most kids experienced in that formative age from their kindergarten teacher. I was a brown, poor, and most likely at-risk child during this time. One of our passage reads, "If a White child has a learning disability, it's real. That's something we need to work with. If it is a Latino or Black child, it's just that they are bad kids (Wilgus, 2014)." This passage speaks exactly to my earliest educational experience.

In the extensive report, "Equity or Marginalization The High School Course-Taking of Students Labeled with a Learning Disability," it provides, "contemporary research suggests that students are more likely to be labeled with an LD (learning disability) if they are from low socio-economic status (SES) households, if they are racial minorities, boys, or language minorities. (Callahan, 2013)." I grew up in a multi-cultural household, where higher education was not something my parents encouraged. Most of their expectations revolved around "not making trouble" for the "aiga" (Samoan word for family) and eventually when the time came, contributing to the household or joining the military. I do not mean to say, education is not valued in Samoan households, it was just something you had to do, but not something I recall aspiring to excel at. Yet in retrospect, I start to think about how unfairly we may have been treated and perhaps, the system was titled in a manner that contributed to feelings of exclusion and "otherness (Loftis, 2015)."

COMPENDIUM: MALINGERING AND DISABILITIES

(In COMPENDIUM: MALINGERING AND DISABILITIES the passage touches on the defensive position individuals may find themselves in when facing suspicion, emphasizing the need to justify their illness. The questioning of the trustworthiness of people claiming to be disabled is highlighted, reflecting the challenges individuals with chronic illnesses face in having their experiences and conditions acknowledged without skepticism. It provides insight into the intersection of military culture, perceptions of illness, and the stigmatization faced by individuals with chronic conditions.)

A TERM THAT I CAME accustomed to while in the military was called "malingering". It is defined as, a "criminal offense of feigning mental or physical illness, or intentionally hurting oneself, in order to avoid military duties (MJA, 2022)". I recalled if someone did not go to work, failed a physical fitness exam, or was sent to sick call, they needed to "really" be sick or injured. Otherwise, if they were not "really" sick they ran the risk of being labeled a malingerer and would suffer the stigma that accompanies it. There are many urban legends that circulate about service members who would shoot themselves in the foot to avoid going to the frontline. In Vietnam that was considered the "million dollar" wound. The rationale involved avoiding the need to risk your life fighting in the jungles of the Viet Cong if you were medically deemed "unfit." Depending on which perspective you hold, having the "million dollar" wound could be a blessing or cowardly.

The articles provided here reminded me well of the stigma I observed while in the military. Wendell writes about the stigma of those with chronic illness endured that takes the form of suspicion. She writes, "suspicion surrounds people with chronic illnesses— suspicion about how ill/disabled we really are, how or why we became ill, whether we are doing everything possible to get well, and how mismanaging our lives, minds, or souls maybe contributing to our continuing illness (Wendell, 2013)." Her depiction reminded me of feeling the need to justify illness because in the service if suspicion evolved around you, at least in my experience, most of the time you would be considered "guilty until proven innocent." The fear of being stigmatized as a malingerer puts you in a defensive position and as Wendell states, "the trustworthiness of people who claim to be disabled (Wendell, 2013)" comes into question.

There is nothing worse than having your integrity questioned for a servicemember.

Back then I did not consider, "why does the stigmatization of malingering resonate so harshly with the military?" Obvious assumptions would have circled back to the warrior ethos they embed in all our training and doctrine. However, in considering Wendell's article, perhaps there is a more ethereal reason why contempt exists in the stigma. In "Disability as Masquerade" by Tobin Seibers, the metaphor of a "closet" is introduced to speak of how disability at times can be covered up or concealed (Siebers, 2004). His root for the metaphor is based in the need to hide something, he equates disability being hidden to the "don't ask, don't tell" policy of the military regarding homosexuality in the 90's (Siebers, 2004). With that in mind, the closet in this case could be hiding fear for individual safety, or the lack of confidence that their safety will be provided.

Perhaps it is in the avoidance of the stigmatization of being weak where the negative attitudes toward being ill or injured arises. The phenomenon of manifesting evil with impairment could come from this place. Eventually this manifestation takes the form of fear. Brown provides, "fears are grounded in a realistic assessment of the negative social consequences of stigmatization and reflect the long-term social and psychological damage to individuals (Brown, 2013)."

I could argue that this fear causes a phenomenon to occur where an evolution takes place that strengthens and entrenches stigma against anyone with seeming illness, injury, disability and perceived weakness. These hardened feelings could be the fuel for self-perpetuating stigmas. Consequently, most people want to ensure that they are counted in the nonstigmatized "majority." This, of course, leads to more stigmatization (Brown, 2013)."

Ultimately, the stigmatization becomes its own generator running on fear. Therefore, I would interpret the use of a "closet" regarding illness or injury in the military as essentially a safe place to be weak or soft located safely away from stigmatization. Sadly, use of closets to avoid stigmas result in actions and decision that drive disastrous behavior for service members, even to the extent of shooting themselves in the foot in order to get a "million dollar" wound.

COMPENDIUM: IDENTITY AND DISABILITIES

(In COMPENDIUM: IDENTITY AND DISABILITIES the passage reflects on the potential dangers of false narratives embedded in identity, citing examples from past elections where narratives were tied to patriotic identity, leading to exclusion and division. The concept of "intellectual tolerance" is proposed to extinguish the flames of anger and division fueled by tribalism and identity. It prompts reflection on the nuanced nature of identity, urging a consideration of shared humanity and intellectual tolerance to mitigate the negative consequences associated with rigid and exclusive identity categories.

SIEBERS STATES, "IF history has taught us anything, it is that those in power have the ability to manipulate the same oppressive structures, dependent upon the same prejudicial representations, for the exclusion of different groups (Siebers, 2013)." This summarized the impression I was left with after reading his article on identity. Although the readings may not have intended to take me down this pessimistic road, I felt a resonating perception of nativism that underlines my concern regarding a wholesale belief in what I am calling the "purity of identity".

Each reading exalted the virtue of having a connection to a specific type of identity to include gender, race and disability. However, it spoke of only the positive things that come from aligning with a centric labeled identity. I have to inquire, "couldn't it also create limitations in terms of setting a ceiling on what you perhaps could evolve into in the future?" If we can accept the premise that the social power dynamic favors those whom society deems as the empowered identity group, therein lies a viable potential for oppression to fester. What stops any particular group from cultivating what Siebers referred to as "prejudicial representations"? With that in mind, I posit whether it is better to avoid grasping and committing to centric identity labels.

Things can change; As Garland prophetically wrote about the identity of being disabled, "disability is the most human of experiences, touching every family and if we live long enough touching us all (Garland-Thomson, 2013)." Furthermore, disability should be considered an equal opportunity employer because "disability is an identity category that anyone can enter at any time, and we will all join it if we live long enough (Garland-Thomson, 2013)." The power dynamic that comes with group identity can swing in favor of or against us at any time, and that is why I caution against believing the panacea for societies injustices comes from committing and locking into only like-minded tribes.

There is a book by Sebastian Junger titled "Tribe: On Homecoming and Belonging", he made the argument about how its in human nature to search for tribes, and in finding these tribes we create our meaning and find our identity. He stated, "If you want to make a society work, then you don't keep underscoring the places where you're different—you underscore your shared humanity (Junger, 2016)." He also provided that tribes have a potential to turn, and they often do.

I witnessed how this occurred in the past election with certain political entities that shaped false narratives but embedded the message into the patriotic identity portrayed by the candidates. I thought to myself, "how to people become so consumed with a false narrative?" Regardless of fact or fiction, belief in the narrative tied into the since of identity. This projected use of identity birthed what Seibers offered as a means to "exclude groups (Siebers, 2013)." Perhaps the way to extinguish the flames of anger and division stoked from tribalism and identity is to practice what Garland provides as "intellectual tolerance" (Garland-Thomson, 2013).

COMPENDIUM: INTERSECTIONALITY AND DISABILITIES

(In COMPENDIUM: INTERSECTIONALITY AND DISABILITIES the passage explores the multifaceted nature of intersectionality, its application in collaborative endeavors, and its role in informing and enriching the author's creative project involving a disabled protagonist. The commitment to empathetic storytelling and the incorporation of intersectional perspectives contribute to a nuanced and inclusive narrative.)

I BELIEVE IF YOU LOOK hard enough, you can find meaning in anything. I don't offer this sarcastically, but as an optimistic point of view. In failure you can find success, in hardship you can find a way forward, and in loss you can find your reason. I have come across this term "intersectionality" a few times in Disabilities Studies. I must admit that I read over it and did not stop to think about it in depth till recently. However, now that I have...I have many self-revelations I did not know existed.

I may have assumed the things that were deemed to be connected in theme or concept were obvious, or I just did not piece the rationale and circumstances together as they were proposed in the narrative. In thinking of the term intersectionality, it takes me back to the concept of "Joint Operations" from my time in the service. The concept of Joint in the military is basically taking the strengths from the respective branches and using them to resolve an issue, campaign, or crisis. It appeals to an assets perspective that not every component has the necessary strengths or skill sets to tackle a problem, though, if you borrow from those that do, you have a better chance of meeting the objectives and completing the mission.

Military speak aside, the concept of intersectionality came up in my Ph.D. application I submitted. They ask pointedly do you have any idea who you could work with outside the school you are applying. To grasp this concept, you need to understand the value of collaboration, as well as have empathy for those with different points of view than your own. Even more important, to really grasp the concept of intersectionality, teamwork and collaboration, I believe you must seek those with starkly contrasting and conceptually conflicting points of view in comparison to the ones you have.

In "Trial of Supercrip", I have taken a rather large bite in developing a character-based script from the perspective of a disabled protagonist. I am writing without any personal experience of the disability my character has, but I believe I was able to cure this through adopting the points of view I have been exposed to through the readings of Disabilities Studies. Themes of alienation, narrative prothesis, and stigma are the types of issues my main character deals with. Thankfully McRuer states, "intersectionality may provide the means for dealing with other marginalizations as well (McRuer, 2017)." And if being marginalized allows you to employ intersectionality, then I believe I can give the characters some empathetic justice in the narrative. Speaking from the perspective of someone who has felt something akin to oppression as a marginalized ethnicity (Samoan), I hope my perspective can fuel intersectional areas in my script and allows for a connection with the reader.

COMPENDIUM: SPIRIT KILLING AND DISABILITIES

(In COMPENDIUM: SPIRIT KILLING AND DISABILITIES the passage explores the concept of "Spirit Killing" discussed in the context of intersectionality and disabilities. It expresses gratitude for gaining improved clarity and connects this notion to the book "1619," where the argument implies that the oppressed are responsible for their own oppression, reflecting a disturbing form of ignorance and injustice.)

IN COMPENDIUM: INTERSECTIONALITY AND DISABILITIY, I explored

the need for establishing a connection, the risk of these connections come to view with the provocative topic of "Spirit Killing" (Minear, 2017) . The horror stories provided by Nirmala Erevelles and Andrea Minear are stirring in many ways. Particularly in light of the holiday of Thanksgiving, where a narrative of being thankful is projected everywhere you turn. Conversely, there should be a counterbalance for being "accountable" for all things we paint as a blessing.

They write a powerful passage about 'Spirit Murdering the Messenger,' Critical Race Feminist (CRF) Patricia Williams describes the brutal murder of a poor, elderly, overweight, disabled, black woman by several heavily armed police officers (Minear, 2017)." Though the injustice Cassie endures in the story may not be the most unique in the scope of all the world's injustices, I find it resonating as an example of how racism, ableism, and classism all intersect and culminate at a flashpoint.

These flashpoints in turn become intersectional experiences by those who understand the feeling of being marginalized and oppressed. With all of this in mind, I am truly thankful for the improved clarity I have now regarding these issues on this Thanksgiving holiday.

> *"It was this same benevolence that allowed the institution to justify the unequal and oppressive conditions in the institution by arguing that "the lack of facilities are not due to racial biases but the fact that Negro patients are willing to accept what is provided to them...*
>
> (Minear, 2017)".

In the book 1619, they mention a quote by Abraham Lincoln that essentially says, we are aware that you have been oppressed with slavery, but you have to understand that you have oppressed us (whites) with your presence here. (Hannah-Jones, 2019) The heavy handedness of the term, "benevolence" is crushing. It speaks to me when I read it, "well we did not want to do this, but you brought this on yourself." Its not about injustice as much as it is about ignorance. It's here were you find the faux nostalgia for when times were better and how good they used to have it. It's a bothersome quote, and I wanted to throw my critical penalty flag at it.

COMPENDIUM: GENDER AND DISABILITIES

(In COMPENDIUM: GENDER AND DISABILITIES the passage provides how Clare's use of metaphors is a coping mechanism, highlighting a passage where she describes roaming beaches and hills, finding solace in stones as the steadiest parts of herself. The metaphors are seen as a means of transforming hardship and pain into visualization and metamorphosis.)

I WAS NOT PREPARED for the ride I went on when I read "Stones in my pocket, stones in my heart" by Eli Clare. I cannot recall any other article from the Disabilities Reader that was as raw and honest as her depiction of the horror she went through with her abuse and what her existence as a "dyke" means to her. I still have some difficulty saying this term, but I feel I need to use the language she intentionally used in her article. If I tried to avoid using the term dyke, then I think I missed the entire point of her story.

I've said it numerous times that I am a child of the 70's; I am a bonafide Gen Xer. My lack of LGBTQ acumen, my ignorant aperture for topics provided in this article, and my astonishment of the graphic narrative provided by Clare were catapulted to the shock and awe realm. Though, I mention this with the preface that if she tried to convene this story in any other fashion, she would have done herself a disservice. What makes writing effective, in my opinion, is the commitment to honesty. The material is beyond sensitive and as personal as an author can get, therefore, using a creative narrative seemed like the best way to bridge her hard story with concrete meaning and purpose.

There was no succumbing to conventional norms. For instance, she wrote "(I) Roamed the beaches at high tide and low, starfish, mussels, barnacles clinging to the rocks. Wandered in the hills thick with moss, fern, liverwort, bramble, tree. Only here did I have a sense of body. Those stones warm in my pockets, I knew them to be the steadiest, only inviolate parts of myself. I wanted to be a hermit, to live alone with my stones and trees, neither a boy nor a girl (Clare, 2013)." This passage is rift with metaphors, and if you spend too much time trying to decipher the meaning, I believe the intent will be lost. Her metaphors are her coping mechanism, by transforming the hardship and pain into visualization and metamorphosis.

As an artist Clare allows us to gain her point of view, and not rustles the audience to serve as poetic interpreters. If that were not the case, this narrative would be like having someone try to interpret a fortune being told by a fortune teller. I do not think that was her intent, she wants us to come along as observers, witnessing her experience, and not trying to get caught up making sense of the analogies and metaphors. That's not our job, I believe the reader's job is to hold testament to her elegy of the horrors and changes she went through in order to survive and give her story.

COMPENDIUM: EPILOUGE

The journey that led to this page, was one I never had thought I would ever take. On a whim or gift of serendipity, I signed up for a course in Disabilities Studies at the University of Hawaii. I had no idea what the course entailed, only that it was appealing to my schedule and there were no prerequisites preventing open enrollment to unclassified graduate students, which I was at the time. At that point in my life, I had recently gotten off a 28-year carrousel of the military, which for lack of a better term, I'll refer to it as a love-hate relationship. For all the great and wonderous opportunities, I was afforded, I also endured some of the darkest times of my life. I ran into demons in every turn, and many of the nemesis I fought, I would soon realize existed in my own lack of awareness of my relationship with disability. To include my brothers who I dedicated this book to, and ultimately my own. Disability was something that I successfully hid from plane site, when multiple clues were laid out for the world to see. Even I was unaware that this was my reality as well.

Writing the story of Cormac and Supercrip started off as an ambitious project, something I wanted to prove to myself that I could do. However, in the end, it resulted in a catharsis of emotions that allowed me to search what being disabled meant to me. As a career officer, I held firm to the warrior ethos, something that devalued weakness as it could degrade the mission and become infectious to my subordinates. I believed that I had to be strong, and even more toxically, I needed to ensure that I was ready to engage with anyone who dared to penetrate this false wall.

As I started to develop this story and write my essays, I began to accept the reality that living with a disability was not about surviving, it became about empowering. I was empowered to accept disability as something I have, and in my case, something that has made me capable to view the world through the lens of neurodiversity. It became my advantage, and when thinking about my brothers, it allowed me to take a break from being angry and ashamed and start to understand the world they lived in was different, but no less valued to them than mine.

I interviewed Dan Frey, the Executive Director of City Voices, the Schizophrenia peer support program I referred to in "COMPENDIUM: ISOLATION AND DISABILITIES," it was one of the most enlightening conversations I ever had, but the thing that resonated the most to me was an interaction we had about my brother. I mentioned to him how I had a rage in me, a need to protect him from others staring at him and wanting to make fun of him. He provided me with one question. He asked, "Does it bother him?" I said, "Of course not, he could care less." Then he asked me, "Then why does it bother you?" Mr. Frey changed my entire perspective with that question. I realized there and then it was about my paradigms, the nemesis was in me.

In "The Trial of Supercrip (And the Conviction of Narrative Prosthesis)," I attempted to present an exploration of disability, identity, and societal tropes. Through the story of Cormac and Supercrip, readers were invited to consider the ways in which societal norms and expectations shaped our understanding of ourselves and others. The play challenged readers to question their assumptions and to see the world through a different lens. My hope is that the story of Cormac and Supercrip is one that is both thought-provoking and emotionally engaging.

Finally, I would be remiss if I did not recognize two very influential people that gave me the empowerment to write this book, Dr. Holly Manaseri and Dr. Rapheal Rapheal, both with the University of Hawaii-Manoa Center for Disabilities Studies. Though they may be unaware of what they did, they instilled in me the confidence to have the courage to write this narrative. Even more important, they were benevolent enough to read, acknowledge and encourage me to continue expressing these thoughts. These were the type of teachers I dreamed of in my youth. Thank you for reading the Trial of Supercrip and the Conviction of Narrative Prosthesis.

Compendium Bibliography

Astor, M. (2022, October 26). How People With Disabilities Saw Fetterman's Debate Performance. *New York Times.*

Barube, M. (2013). Disability, Democracy, and the New Genetics. In L. J. Davis, *The Disabilities Reader* (pp. 101-114). New York: Routledge.

Beckett, S. (1954). *Waiting for Godot: A tragic comedy in two acts.* New York: Grove Press.

Ben-Moshe, L. (2013). "The Institution Yet to Come": Analyzing Incarceration Through a

Disability Lens. In L. J. Davis, *The Disabilities Reader* (pp. 132-143). New York: Routledge.

Blaustein, B. W. (Director). (2005). *The Ringer* [Motion Picture].

Brown, L. C. (2013). Stigma: An Enigma Demystied. In L. J. Davis, *The Disabilities Reader* (pp. 147-160). New York City: Routledge.

Callahan, D. S. (2013). Equity or Marginalization? The High School Course-Taking of Students Labeled with a Learning Disability. *American Educational Research Journal*, 656-682.

Clare, E. (2013). Stones in My Pockets, Stones in My Heart. In L. J. Davis, *The Disabilities Reader* (pp. 497-506). New York City: Routledge.

Couser, G. T. (2005). Disability, Life Narrative, and Representation. *Publications of the Modern Language Association of America*, 602-606.

Davis, L. J. (2013). *Reader, The Disability Studies*. (Fourth, Ed.) New York, NY: Routledge.

Davis, L. J. (2017). The Ghettoization of Disability: Paradoxes of Visibility and Invisibility in Cinema. In H. B. Anne Waldschmidt, *Culture – Theory – Disability: Encounters between Disability Studies and Cultural Studies* (pp. 30-49). Germany: Bielefeld transcript Verlag.

Emens, E. (2013). Disabling Attitudes: U.S. Disability Law asnd the ADA Amendments. In L. Davis, *The Disabilities Reader* (pp. 205-233). New York: Routledge.

Feig, P. (Director). (2005). *Arrested Development: The Ocean Walker* [Motion Picture]. Retrieved from https://www.youtube.com/ watch?v=dEmyHOZTtFc

Garland-Thomson, R. (2002). The Politics of Staring:Visual Rhetorics of Disability in Popular Photography. In S. L.-T. Snyder, *Disability Studies: Enabling the Humanities* (pp. 56-75). New York: Modern Language Association of America.

Garland-Thomson, R. (2013). Integrating Disability, Transforming Feminist Theory. In L. J. Davis, *The Disability Studies Reader* (pp. 333-353). New York City: Routledge.

Hahn, H. (1987). *Civil Rights For Disabled Americans: The Foundation of a Political Agenda.* Farsta: Independent Living Institute.

Hannah-Jones, N. E. (2019). *The 1619 Project.* New York City: New York Times.

Johnson, J. R. (2006). Validation and Affirmation of Disability and Deaf Culture: A Content Analysis of Introductory Textbooks to Special Education and

Exceptionality. *Review of Disability Studies An International Journal*, 3-32.

Junger, S. (2016). *Tribe: On Homecoming and Belonging.* New York: Hachette Book Group.

Kittay, E. F. (2015). Centering Justice on Dependency and Recovering Freedom. *Hypatia, Vol. 30, No. 1, SPECIAL ISSUE: New Conversations in Feminist Disability*, 285-291.

Kwik, J. (2020). *Limitless: Upgrade Your Brain, Learn Anything Faster, and Unlock Your Exceptional Life.* Hay House.

LeBesco, K. (2004, Summer). There's Something About Disabled People: The Contradictions of Freakery in the Films of the Farrelly Brothers. *Disabilities Studies Quarterly, 24*(4), 1-8.

Lewis, B. (2013). A Mad Fight: Psychiatry and Disability Activism. In L. J. Davis, *The Disabilities Reader* (pp. 115-131). New York: Routledge.

Linton, S. (1998). *Claiming Disabilit.* New York: New York University Press.

Loftis, S. F. (2015). The Autistic Victim: Of Mice and Men and Flowers for Algernon. In S. F. Loftis, *In Imagining Autism* (pp. 61-78). Bloomington: Indiana University Press.

Longmore, P. K. (2003). Screening Stereotypes: Images of Disabled People in Television and Motion Pictures . In P. K. Longmore, *Why I Burned My Book, and other essays on disability* (pp. 131-146). Philadelphia: Temple University Press.

McCarthy, C. (1985). *Blood Meridian or The Evening Redness In the West.* New York: Vintage Books.

McRuer, R. (2017). Compulsory Able-Bodiedness and Queer Disabled Existence. In L. J. Davis, *The Disability Studies Reader* (pp. 397-406). New York City: Routledge.

Meekosha, H. a. (2009). What's So Critical About Critical Disability Studies? *Australian Journal of Human Rights*, 15.

Minear, N. E. (2017). Unspeakable Offenses: Untangling Race and Disability in Discourses of Intersectionality. In L. J. Davis, *The Disabiities Reader* (pp. 381-395). New York City: Routledge.

MJA. (2022). *Understanding Article 83, UCMJ – Malingering.* Retrieved from MIlitary Justice Attorneys: https://www.militaryjusticeattorneys.com/blog/understanding-article-83-ucmj-malingering/#:~:text=%E2%80%9CMalingering%E2%80%9D%

Murray, H.-D. L. (2013). Deaf Studies in the 21st Century Deaf Gain and the Future of Human Diversity. In L. J. Davis, *Reader, The Disability Studies* (pp. 253-260). New York: Routledge.

Pacific Standard Staff. (2013, July 22). *THERE'S A NAME FOR THAT: THE BAADER-MEINHOF PHENOMENON*. Retrieved from Pacific Standard Staff: https://psmag.com/social-justice/theres-a-name-for-that-the-baader-meinhof-phenomenon-59670

Prendergast, C. (2013). The Unexceptional Schizophrenic: A PostPostmodern Introduction. In L. J. Davis, *Reader, The Disability Studies* (pp. 243-252). New York: Routledge.

Price, M. (2013). Defining Mental Disability. In L. J. Davis, *The Disabilities Reader* (pp. 209-307). New York City: Routledge.

Putnam, R. D. (2000). *Bowling Alone: the Collapse and Revival of American Community*. New York: Simon & Schuster.

Quayson, A. (2013). Aesthetic Nervousness. In L. J. Davis, *The Disability Studies Reader* (pp. 208-219). New York: Routledge.

Raphael, R. (2012). Teaching Film and Disability Studies. In L. F. Petro, *Teaching Film (Options for*

Teaching) (pp. 74-86). Modern Language Association.

Sandahl, C. (2008). Why Disability Identity Matters: From Dramaturgy to Casting in John Belluso's Pyretown. *Text and Performance Quarterly, Vol. 28, Nos. 102,* 225-241.

Saxton, M. (2013). Disability Rights and Selective Abortion. In L. J. Davis, *The Disabilities Studies Reader* (pp. 87-99). New York: Routledge.

Shakespere, T. (2013). The Social Model of Disability. In L. Davis, *The Disability Studies Reader* (pp. 214-221). New York: Routledge.

Shuttleworth, H. (2009). What's so Critical About Critical Disabilities Studies? *Australian Journal of Human Rights, 15.*

Siebers, T. (2004). Disability as Masquerade. *Literature and Medicine,* 1-22.

Siebers, T. (2013). Disability and the Theory of Complex Embodiment—For Identity Politics in a New Register. In L. J. Davis, *The Disability Studies Reader* (pp. 278-297). New York City: Routledge.

Snyder, D. M. (2013). Narrative Prosthesis. In L. J. Davis, *The Disabilities Studies Reader* (pp. 222-235). New York: Routledge.

USAF. (2023, August 18). Air Force Instruction 1-1: Air Force Standards. *Department of the Air Force.*

Voices, C. (2022, September 10). *Media and Community-building Projects.* Retrieved from City Voices Online: https://www.cityvoicesonline.org/about/

Wendell, S. (2013). Unhealthy Disabled: Treating Chronic. In L. J. Davis, *The Disability Studies Reader* (pp. 161-173). New York City: Routledge.

Wilgus, G. V. (2014). Algorithms of Access: Immigrant Mothers Negotiating Educational Resources and Services for their Children. *Review of Disability Studies An International Journal,* 88-102.

---

[1] DR RAPHAEL RAPHEAL, is an Associate Professor at the University of Hawaii, references an orientation video he provided for his Disabilities Studies Course.

Did you love *The Trial of Supercrip (And the Conviction of Narrative Prosthesis)*? Then you should read *Triggers of Aggression in Crowds; The Milieu of High School Football*[1] by James Faumuina!

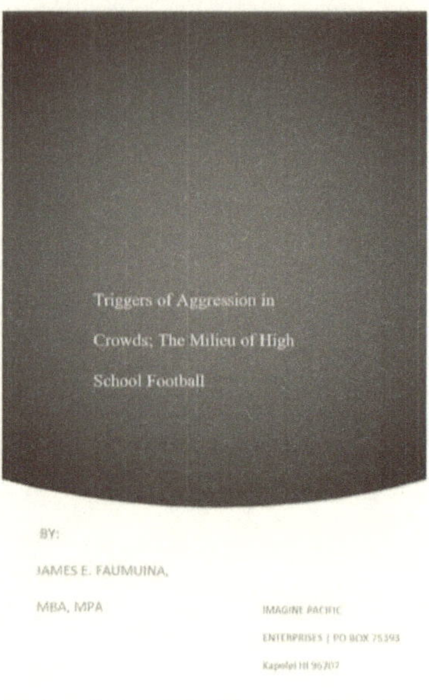

Over the course of a season, observations were made of eight teams from eight different schools on the island of Oahu. The attempt to capture aggression triggers in crowd derived three concrete themes: 1) Cohesion is a tangible entity that can be identified and is possibly the spark in group aggressive behavior, 2) Voluntary and involuntary conditioned response are spurred by unscripted activities taking place during the

---

1. https://books2read.com/u/4X2zX1

2. https://books2read.com/u/4X2zX1

games, 3) Schools that utilized structure did so deliberately to avoid or diffuse aggression in crowds. In pursuit of aggressive triggers the overarching lessons illuminated, the context drives the impression of the severity and validity of the aggression observed. Impressively there are those who are adept at facilitating the context with the triggers of aggression, and conversely there are those who blindly fall into the movement of the crowd as aggression turns contagious.

About the Author

James E. Faumuina retired from the Hawaii Air National Guard, notably overseeing the state's first CBRNE and All Hazards Medical response unit. Concurrently, he is pursuing a Ph.D. in the Troy Global Studies Program and a Graduate Certificate in Disabilities and Diversified Studies at the University of Hawaii Manoa. With a foundation in psychology, he is the owner of Imagine Pacific Enterprises, and this is his second book. He also authored the "Triggers of Aggression in Crowds: The Milieu of High School Football" in 2021.

Read more at https://imagine-pacific.com/.

About the Publisher

Imagine Pacific Enterprises
  PO Box 75393
  Kapolei, HI 96707
  (B) 808-674-0520
  Email: Administrator@imagine-pacific.com